THE
MILLIONAIRE
dropout

THE
MILLIONAIRE
dropout

FIRE YOUR BOSS. DO WHAT YOU LOVE.
RECLAIM YOUR LIFE!

Vince Stanzione

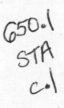
WILEY

Published by John Wiley & Sons, Inc., Hoboken, New Jersey.
Published simultaneously in Canada.

For general information about our other products and services, please contact our Customer Care
Department within the United States at (800) 762-2974, outside the United States at (317) 572-3993
or fax (317) 572-4002.

Wiley publishes in a variety of print and electronic formats and by print-on-demand. Some material
included with standard print versions of this book may not be included in e-books or in print-on-
demand. If this book refers to media such as a CD or DVD that is not included in the version you
purchased, you may download this material at http://booksupport.wiley.com. For more information
about Wiley products, visit www.wiley.com.

Library of Congress Cataloging-in-Publication Data:

Stanzione, Vince.
    The millionaire dropout: fire your boss. do what you love. reclaim your life! / Vince Stanzione.
        pages cm
    Includes index.
    ISBN 978-1-118-60948-4 (pbk.); ISBN 978-1-118-65283-1 (ebk); ISBN 978-1-118-65277-0
(ebk); ISBN 978-1-118-65268-8 (ebk)
    1. Success.   2. Success in business.   3. Self-actualization (Psychology)
    4. Job satisfaction. I.   Title.
    BF637.S8S687 2013
    650.1–dc23   2013001364

Contents

Acknowledgments

My thanks to:

Mark Anastasi (http://www.laptopmillionaire.tv) for some great advice and introductions.

Bill Myers (http://www.bmyers.com), the original free thinker who helped me realize life isn't all about making more money.

Ted Nicholas (http://www.Tednicholas.com) for teaching me the power of words and copywriting.

John Caples and David Ogilvy, whose books taught me the power of advertising and direct mail.

Susanna Quinn for editing this book and JLS for your honest opinions and priceless support.

Lastly, and most importantly, a big thank you to all the readers, clients, and business partners who made everything possible over the last 28 years.

Preface

This Book Isn't About Me, It's About You

If you're reading this online, or flipping pages in a bookshop, thinking *Why should I buy this book?*, then let me tell you. I can help *you* have an amazing life. I haven't written this book to impress you, but to impress upon you what a nonacademic, near bankrupt, occasionally homeless social dropout can achieve in a relatively short period of time.

I haven't written this book to make money. I'm already a multi-millionaire, and have been for many years.

This is a school of hard knocks how-to manual, and there is no exam or fancy degree at the end. But if you follow my advice and take action, you can live a lifestyle others only dream about. You can join the new rich—and I don't mean only rich in money. I mean rich in time and fulfillment.

But let's go back a few years . . . I didn't come from a privileged or well-educated background. My father came to the United Kingdom from a small, poor town in South Italy. He was escaping the mafia, and had nothing but a battered case and a few shillings. He couldn't speak a word of English.

By working as a hairdresser by day and a waiter by night (I know . . . all Italians are hairdressers or waiters!), he made enough to start his own hairdressing salon and built up a successful chain.

He then retired and dropped dead a few years later, at the relatively young age of 55. I had no interest in joining the family business, but I did share the family ethos of hard work.

At the age of 12, I was doing payroll for the hair salons, washing hair, and cleaning. However, I knew I wanted a business of my own.

I set up my first mail-order business at that age, selling computer games stored on tapes. Remember the Commodore 64 and ZX Spectrum?

I was the fairly quiet kid who never fit in. We moved around a lot, so I was always the new kid at school. I was badly bullied for years, and teased for being overweight and having the wrong accent.

I had about every illness you could think of—including serious asthma, eczema so bad that I struggled to hold a pen, and sight problems that meant I couldn't see the board at school.

The only thing I liked about school was selling stuff to other kids (and a few teachers too).

At 16, I landed my first job—as a junior in a Foreign Exchange Dealing Room. This paid £100 ($150) a week, and was an awful job.

I was treated like dirt by the dealers (many of whom took drugs and smoked 60 cigarettes a day), but because I didn't want to become a hairdresser I stuck it out. I learned how to trade financial markets and read everything I could at the local library.

I ate the dealer's leftovers in the staff canteen, and owned one cheap Marks & Spencer gray polyester suit that stank of smoke.

Within six months I was promoted, and within two years I was dealing multimillion-dollar positions. I then moved into equities, and traded for others and myself.

Life was good. I was living the Thatcher dream—or so I thought. Then the 1987 crash wiped me out, and I lost everything. In fact, more than everything. I was ready to be declared bankrupt by my ex-employer, who wanted to claw back commission. Luckily, the judge felt sorry for me and threw the case out on the grounds that I had no money to pay.

I then worked various commission-only jobs to get a bit of income. I started my own business selling car phones, and then mobile phones.

Working from a studio apartment, I built that business up from one newspaper ad, merged it with another dealership, and sold my share for a substantial sum a few years later.

The truth is, it was worth a lot more than I sold it for, but considering I was only 21 and had nearly been declared bankrupt not so long ago, it felt like an amazing sum of money.

I bought my first Rolex watch, which I still own today—not to show off, but because I knew if I was ever hard up and needed to start again, I could pawn it. Fortunately, I never had to.

So what can you learn from a millionaire dropout? I don't claim to have all the answers. I don't claim that every business or every investment I've made has been successful. However, I do know that if I share my secrets, *you* will be successful and avoid many of my mistakes.

Along my journey, from selling computer games on tape, to washing hair, to dealing currencies, to standing in bankruptcy court, to sleeping in a Ford van, to being forced to use a credit card to pay the staff, to escaping from the Russian mafia (trust me, you can't make this up!), to floating a business on the London Stock Exchange, to making millions in sales, I have picked up a few tips and secrets. If I can pass on just a few of those to you, I am certain you'll cover the cost of this book many times over.

Do you want to come on a journey with me?

I sincerely hope so.

—Vince Stanzione
The Millionaire Dropout

Introduction

YOU ONLY LIVE ONCE, AT least on this planet. So let me ask you this. Are you making the best of your life, earning plenty of money, and feeling relaxed, happy, and content? Or are you trudging through each day, waiting for life to get better?

If you can truly say you're happy with the quality of your life, the amount of money you earn, and your relationships, then read no further. I congratulate you and would love to learn your secrets.

If, however, you're one of the millions who hate getting up in the morning and earning a meager wage at a job you loathe, only to find your paycheck has run out 25 days before payday, read on.

This book has been written for all those who want to boost their income, reduce their outgoings, and increase their standard of living. Whether you're young, old, previously successful, or have never had any success, I will show you how to create an amazing life that you will love living.

The book is divided into three sections:

Part I Taking Control of Your Life

First, we will focus on you—your goals, fears, past, state-of-mind, and how to take control of all these things to start living every day to its full potential. I will teach you how to reprogram your mind for success, and transform your mood and appearance through diet and exercise. You will finish this section charged-up and ready to learn the secrets of making money.

Part II Making Money

I will reveal my money-making secrets, and show how you can copy tried-and-tested formulas to make as much money as you want and deserve. I'll also explain how to get a pay raise and start earning your true worth.

Part III Saving Money

Smart people are good at both making money and saving money. No matter how wealthy you are, it always pays to buy everything at the lowest possible price, and I'll show you how. Whether you're buying a car, toaster, designer dress, or the latest gadget, I will reveal how to get the best deal.

There Is a Better Life for You

I don't know what your current position is, but I can guess you want more than you currently have. Perhaps you have money worries or debts and feel that you need or deserve a higher income. Or maybe you have a string of failed relationships and feel uncertain about the future. Somehow, life is passing you by, and although you know you should be doing better, you're stuck in a rut and not living, but scarcely existing.

The good news is there is a better life. You can increase your income, pay off debts, and—most importantly—increase your quality of life and gain self-confidence and respect. You genuinely can have everything in the world that you really want. And I will show you how.

Always Remember—It Could Be Worse

I can tell you truthfully that however bad your situation is—whether you're in debt, have personal difficulties, low self-esteem, or are addicted to drugs or alcohol—I can guarantee you're not alone and there is a way out.

I want you to remember this:

You may be crying and upset because you haven't any shoes, but spare a thought for the person next to you. He hasn't any feet.

And that's your first lesson. It may look bad, but believe me—it could be worse.

Only You Can Change Your Life for the Better

You are in charge of your life. Everything that's happened to you in the past—your successes, failures, and problems—were brought about by your actions (or lack of them) in one way or another.

I know the truth hurts, but this book is about getting results and not just telling you what you want to hear.

It's easy for us to blame other people for our failures, problems, and shortcomings. How many times do you hear people say: "It's my boss's fault . . . my wife's fault . . . if only I was older/younger . . . I blame the government . . . "?

The truth is that *you* are in charge of your life. You're the driver of the train, and you can either choose to drive around the world on a rich, fulfilling, and rewarding journey, or leave the train standing in the station, with the wheels rusting away and the engine seizing up.

I believe we live in amazing times, with an abundance of opportunities. You may not agree, and I can understand why. Every day, the media is full of doom and gloom about the bad economy, and what terrible things are happening in the world.

The truth is, with advances in technology it's never been easier to achieve your financial and lifestyle goals. And it gets easier every day.

But back to the train . . .

You choose: 95 percent of the population are at the station. Are you in that 95 percent? Are you standing still, watching life pass you by?

If you believe in safety in numbers, then stay exactly where you are. Go with the flow, and stick with the masses. If, however, you want to join the 5 percent of people who are driving their trains to amazing places, keep on reading. This book will help you get the train started, and once you get going, you'll be amazed that you were ever standing still.

I'm not saying you'll go flying out of the station at 100 mph, but even if you start to pull away at 1 mph, that's faster than the 95 percent who are standing still. Right?

Do You Really Want Life to Change?

You can do anything you set your mind to—earn lots of money, give up smoking, drugs or alcohol, get into shape—but only if *you* really want your life to change.

This book can help make your life better, but only if you work with the advice given in these pages and take action. I can reveal my wealth secrets to you, but ultimately only you can put those secrets into action and make things happen in your life.

I guarantee that if you want a better life badly enough, this book will help you achieve it.

Some years ago a baseball manager, Tommy Lasorda, said "There are those who watch things happen, those who wonder what happened, and those who make things happen."

Which person are you—a watcher or a player? You need to become a player to win in life. Being a spectator and watching the world go by just isn't any fun. Others may be content to exist and get by being a government chart statistic, but I know that you're not satisfied with being a number. You want to do better than that.

I'm Very Unlucky

I come from a background that believes you make your own luck. If you work 14 hours a day, it's amazing how lucky you will become. Luck is determined by our own efforts—the blood, sweat, and tears we put into life.

I'm sorry, but I don't believe luck has anything to do with whether Jupiter is in Mars, or this year is the Chinese animal year I was born under, or my horoscope in the daily downmarket newspaper says today will be good for finances.

I have done a fair amount of research into luck over the last few years and had the pleasure of meeting Professor Richard Wiseman, author of *The Luck Factor*. He points to four main areas that separate "lucky people" and "unlucky" ones:

1. Lucky people are good at creating chance opportunities.
2. They are good at thinking lucky.
3. They are good at feeling lucky.
4. They believe in denying fate.

I don't like the term *opportunity knocks*. I have found in 99 percent of cases, it doesn't. If you're sitting at home, waiting for opportunities to ring the doorbell, I'm sorry to say this is very unlikely.

You make your own luck in this world, and mine was created by going out and searching high and low for opportunities. If you start creating opportunities, it's amazing how often you will be in the right place at the right time and how lucky you will become.

THE
MILLIONAIRE
dropout

PART

I

Taking Control of Your Life

1

Getting Started

CHANGING YOUR LIFE WILL TAKE effort, perseverance, and time. Most people spend 20 to 30 years messing up their lives. They overeat, overdrink, don't save for the future, don't learn new skills, let their minds cease up, and then hope life will change without them lifting a finger.

The truth is that success and riches come to those who take action and then put in the hours. A steady amount of effort is far better than a short burst and then nothing. It is a fact that the only way to lose weight is by a steady diet, and not a get-slim-quick regime. The old Chinese proverb, "A journey of a million miles begins with one step," is very true in these circumstances. Take your time, but take that first step.

Making money and increasing the quality of your life is similar to being on a diet. You'll have high points and low points, but the key is to keep going and not give up.

Tiny Steps Lead to Massive Leaps

Success normally comes, not from one big change or action, but from lots of small successes that build into a big success. Remember this as you work through the book. Steps that may seem stupid, pointless, and meaningless on their own will combine to make massive leaps forward in your life.

Imagine a brick. A brick on its own is not very exciting, stylish, or useful, but when thousands or millions of bricks are put together, they create amazing buildings.

You often hear a famous actor called an overnight success, but the truth is, there is no such thing. I know many stars are deeply offended by this term, since most work for years in the background before their big break. They build up small successes, such as TV commercials, small background parts, and theater roles, and all this hard work eventually leads to a major part. This is a great example of the small successes leading to a big success.

Can You Go the Extra Mile?

I'm guessing the truthful answer to this question right now is no. However, over time and with the help of this book, we must change that answer to yes.

If you look at life's winners, whether they are great businesspeople, sports people, or show business celebrities, one of their strongest attributes will be their ability to go the extra mile.

Imagine you are a salesman. You've been out all day knocking on doors without any success. It's getting late, and you're tired. Do you give up and go home, or try those extra few doors? It could be that behind those extra doors is the commission you've been working all day for.

Successful inventors are very good at going the extra mile. Many top inventors and scientists kept going, even when everyone told them not to. The end result? An amazing new invention or discovery.

Famous explorers are well-known for their successes, but what most people don't know is that they have many failed explorations, too. However, I've observed that successful explorers don't let these failures stop them. As soon as one attempt fails, they plan their next attempt. They don't give up, and eventually one of their explorations is a success.

Many bestselling items we use every day were called stupid or useless at one time or another. If that inventor had given up because he had been rejected, all his hard work would have been wasted.

Do you know that many top-selling bands, like the Beatles and U2, were turned down by several major record labels? The Beatles were told they were losers and would never last, and we all know what happened to them!

When you go the extra mile, you will stand out and shine. Today, most people try to get by with the minimum amount of work or effort. That's why when someone goes the extra mile—especially in the service industry—the effort really stands out. I'll talk more about this later.

Now let's get back to you. As you read this book, you will be asked to put various plans into action. You will be asked to change the way you act and think.

You may meet resistance from the people around you, as they sense you are trying to change your life. They may accuse you of being stupid or insane, and advise you to give up. When things don't seem to be working out, they may say, "I told you it wouldn't work."

Like the famous inventors and explorers of history, you must learn to ignore these people. Stick to the plans outlined in this book and I guarantee you will prove them all wrong. People may put you down today, but when you drive past them in your new shiny Ferrari and they're standing at the bus stop, I guarantee you will be laughing louder.

Your present circumstances don't determine where you can go; they merely determine where you start.

—Nido Qubein

Breaking Free from Your Comfort Zone

Right now, you are living in your comfort zone. This is what you are familiar with, and—if you're like most people—it involves commuting to a job you'd rather not do, then commuting home, watching TV, sleeping, and starting all over again. On the weekends, you do what you can with your meager pay, including buying a lottery ticket.

Most people see this as a normal and acceptable way to live.

What a waste of a life; yet millions of people are living (or *existing*) like this as you read this book.

Here's a quote to think about:

I go to work, I earn my bread,
　　I watch TV and go to bed,
　　　Sunrise, sunset—year to year,
　　　Before I know it, winter's here.

—*Denis Waitley*

This may sound harsh, but if you're truly honest with yourself, you will agree that 95 percent of the population live like this, possibly including yourself. Go to a train station during rush hour and see people running around like headless chickens. Look at the way they dress, their postures, their facial expressions. You can feel and smell the stress and pollution in the air. Is this the way you want to live?

Of course not! So why are you? Because you are stuck in your comfort zone, and can't imagine a different life.

We stay in our comfort zone because it feels normal to us, and we're scared of failure, embarrassment, and change. The majority of people accept a life that isn't great, and deep down believe that dreams, goals, and desires will only cause pain. They have lost all hopes of being a billionaire—they just want to earn a living and get by.

Benjamin Franklin once said, "Most men die at 25. We just don't bury them until they are 70."

Harsh but true. This is life in the comfort zone. Most of us have been brainwashed by parents, friends, teachers, the media, and our bosses to believe it's okay not to strive or achieve, and that it's better to stay exactly where we are.

If you're brave enough to break free of your comfort zone, I guarantee this book will improve your life. You can and will do better than you are doing today. I want you to be unhappy with your comfort zone. It's time for you to change and act. I want you to dream and reach for the stars. Today is the first day of your new life.

When you reach for the stars, you may not quite get one, but you won't come up with a handful of mud either.

—Leo Burnett

Why I Want You to Succeed

Let me share a secret of successful people. We offer products and services that actually work and improve people's lives. If this book makes you a success, then you'll tell other people, and my sales will increase. If this book doesn't work for you, then you'll be unlikely to tell anyone about it, and probably won't purchase any more of my books or DVDs.

I believe success is always a good thing, and that other people's success will not affect me in any negative way.

This book is a win-win partnership. I really do want you to succeed and be happy.

As you change your life, there will be times when it feels as though it's you against the rest of the world. Remember that in me and this book you have a partner. I am on your side. So there's two of us against the rest of the world, and together I promise we can achieve anything.

Before we get started, I want to apologize in advance if I sound arrogant, rude, or harsh in any of the following text. I need to shake you loose of your negative thoughts and fire you into action—and this may require a kick in the rear.

I would also like to point out that I am the most equal-minded person you will ever meet. I want everyone to be a success, whether you are a man, woman, Black, Asian, green, pink, or whatever, so when I state "Him," "He" or "Man," and so on, it could equally be "Her," "She," or "Women," and so on.

We're Here to Learn, Not Have Fun

If I had a dollar for every time I was told, "We're here to learn, not have fun," when I was at school, I would be a billionaire. Did you hear something similar when you were at school?

When I became an employee, it was the same again. "You're here to work, not mess around."

It sends a very clear message, doesn't it? Doing something worth-while, like learning or earning money, isn't fun.

Well, I'm here to rebel. I believe you can learn, work, and have fun. In fact, I believe that if it's fun, it gets done. That's why this book is informative, but fun, too. So if you're not smiling right now, read the following, and see if you can lighten your mood a little:

Have you ever said something that doesn't quite come out how you meant it? Here are a few true quotes written on motor vehicle insurance forms or statements made to the police:

"Coming home, I drove into the wrong house and collided with a tree I don't have."

"I had been driving my car for 40 years when I fell asleep at the wheel and had an accident."

Here's my favorite, apparently given to the police:

"The guy was all over the road. I had to swerve a number of times before I finally managed to hit him."

I hope you're smiling, at least a little.

The quicker that the learning-and-working-can-be-fun mentality sinks in, the quicker you'll finish this book and start creating success in your life.

So let's get started.

2

Let's Talk About You

WE'RE GOING TO TALK ABOUT the most important person in the world. *You*. Unless you get in the right frame of mind, it's pointless trying to make or save money.

Many of the techniques discussed in Parts II and III will only work once you are feeling strong and have clearly outlined your goals, wants, and needs. *Do not skip this section*.

If you skip this section, you may as well put the book down right now. Yes, you're eager to start, but we need to build strong foundations. Without strong foundations, it doesn't matter how well the building is designed and put together—it will fall down.

I have a question for you. How much do you think you're worth?

   a. 1 million dollars
   b. 10 million dollars
   c. 100 million dollars

Before you answer this question, let me make you an offer. Let's imagine I'm a body broker. I buy and sell body parts such as eyes, legs, hearts, and so on. Now imagine I offered you 10 million dollars for your eyes and another 10 million dollars for your legs. Would you sell me your eyes and legs?

The answer is *no*. Of course not. No amount of money could buy these things.

So how much are you worth? The answer is none of the above. You are priceless—a unique person, with a better brain than the most powerful computer in the world. Even with great new technology and modern microprocessors, computers cannot compete with you.

Your biggest asset is that you are the original, one and only. Of the 6.9 billion people currently inhabiting the earth, there never has been, and never will be, another *you*.

You are truly an incredibly sophisticated creation. Let me tell you a few facts about yourself:

Your body has the capability to repair itself continually at the rate of 2 billion cells per day. (Don't you wish that dent in your car could do that?)

Ninety-eight percent of the atoms in your body change in less than one year. More specifically, you change:

Your skin about every 20 days.

Your stomach about once a month.

All of your brain cells every year and your skeleton once every three months.

Just think. By the time you've finished reading this book, you will be a new person—both in mind and body. So if you want a new start, well—you already have it!

A few other things about yourself:

Your brain has limitless capacity to store and process information.

You have about 600 muscles.

You have about 200 bones.

You have about 20 square feet of skin.

Your heart beats about 100,000 times per day.

Your kidneys will remove 1 million gallons of waste products from your blood by the time you are 70 years of age.

The most expensive, rarest, beautiful, and precious asset that you will ever own is not a painting, piece of jewelry or anything else.

It's *you.*

Now I want to teach you an important lesson in self-confidence. Regardless of your past failures or current difficulties, you can and must believe in yourself.

If you don't believe in yourself, you will never be able to convince anyone else to believe in you.

I've worked in banking in the past, and turned down many business-loan applications for the simple reason that the applicant didn't believe in himself or his new business. If you don't believe in yourself, how can you convince a bank, or anyone else, to back you?

Remembering you are valuable and unique is the antidote to criticism and depression. The next time someone puts you down, or you feel sorry for yourself, remember how precious you truly are. Write this on a piece of paper in big letters, and read it over a few times:

The most expensive, rarest, beautiful, and precious asset I will ever own is ME.

Feeling better? Good. You should. Feeling positive about yourself inspires the confidence you must have to do well in life.

The aim of this section is to make you:

a. Start feeling more successful
b. Act as if you are more successful

The combination of a + b = You will be more successful

Time for Some Surgery

No, I don't mean cosmetic surgery. I mean surgery from within— changing the way you look and feel about yourself.

Let's start with the way you act and present yourself to others, whether it's in person or on the telephone. Here are the important qualities you need to present yourself well.

A Smile

A smile can get you a long way. You can even hear a smile on the telephone. If you ask for something with a smile, there's a far better chance you'll get it than if you look glum and grumpy. Smiling is a positive statement about yourself. It gives others confidence and implies success. The great thing about a smile is that it is international. I can't speak Japanese, but if I walked into a room of Japanese-speaking business people, I could smile, and they would have positive feelings towards me.

One well-known telesales company puts mirrors on its staff's desks, so salespeople can see their facial expressions while they're selling. Apparently sales are soaring.

A Warm, Rich Tone to Your Voice

To be able to speak in public is a very desirable asset, but like everything worthwhile it takes practice and courage.

The way you speak can either help or hurt you. I'm not saying you should try to speak like the queen. That would be false—unless you actually are the queen. Nor should you change your accent. What I do recommend is:

Try to speak clearly, without cutting words short. Speak too quickly, and you'll sound nervous. Speak too slowly, and you'll sound boring and may annoy people.

Practice your speech by recording it on your mobile phone or Dictaphone and listen back.

If you're not naturally a good speaker, it would be wise to invest in one of the many books or DVDs dedicated to this subject. There are also free clips on YouTube that give tips on public speaking. If speaking is a real stumbling block, consider enrolling in a public speaking class. This is an excellent way to improve both your speech and all-round confidence.

We live in a media age, and I guarantee that clear speech is a huge asset. As a highly successful person, the chances are you'll appear on television, radio, or YouTube at some point. In the meantime, you'll speak on the telephone at least a few times a week, and a good, clear voice will be of great benefit.

It's very important to be able to use the telephone effectively, whether you're booking a reservation for a hotel or selling something. Never underestimate the importance of your telephone manner.

I've sold hundreds of thousands of pounds' worth of products over the phone, ranging from computer software, to stocks and shares, and the best tip I can give you is to stand up or walk a few paces while you're talking. Trust me, it makes a difference.

With Skype and teleconferencing services such as Gotomeeting. com, we are now using the telephone more than ever before. Most of us aren't taught how important telephone skills are, or given the opportunity to learn them. Go the extra mile—take the time to practice your telephone manner, and instantly you'll be ahead of most people in life.

Enthusiasm in What You Request

Don't sound unsure or timid, even if you are. Ask for the product/service you require with enthusiasm, and nine times out of ten you'll get it. Trust me, enthusiasm works.

Good Eye Contact

People who don't look others in the eye are seen as shifty and dishonest. It's important to maintain good eye contact with others. This is an easy thing to do with practice.

If you're holding a web meeting, make sure the camera is at eye level or a bit higher, and look straight into the camera, not at the person on screen. If you're on a laptop with a built-in camera, prop it on a few books so that the camera is at eye level.

A Firm Handshake

In the age of video conferencing and e-mail, it's easy to forget about a handshake. But it remains as important as ever. When you're introduced to someone for the first time, a firm handshake gives the very best impression. Whether you are male or female, you should not be afraid to shake hands firmly.

Sincerity and Interest in Others—You Can't Fake Friendliness

This is a very important quality, and without question it helps you get what you want in life. Every day, you will come across people who can make a big difference to your comfort and success. These include hotel desk clerks, airline check-in staff, waiters, office clerks, and sales people, to name a few.

In Part III, you will see how these people can make the difference between flying in the worst seat in economy, or the best seat in first class, so take note.

Most of us treat the "little" people with no respect or dignity. Show some interest in the people you interact with, whether they be a shop assistant, taxi driver, or bartender, and you'll reap the rewards.

You don't have to be false, but look cheerful and ask a few questions to show your interest in others. These questions needn't be too taxing. Saying "It looks busy/quiet today" or "You're working late/early today" is a great way to show you care about someone else's life.

Why bother? First, it's courteous to your fellow human being, and second, if the clerk can offer an upgrade, better product, or way to save money, who will he think of first? The person who looks friendly and takes an interest, or the person who treats him as though he were invisible?

Every time you talk to someone new, either in person or by phone or e-mail, you have the opportunity to sell yourself. You'll never get along with 100 percent of the population, but you can try and beat the averages.

A *Purposeful Posture*

Stand tall, no matter what your height, and you will communicate that you deserve and expect respect.

I've read that taller people are more successful in life, and this may have some truth. However, I believe a purposeful posture is more important than your height. Walking tall and sitting well communicates confidence and success to others. It also helps you speak more clearly and prevents back pains later on in life.

Ensure that your head is held high and your eyes look straight ahead or up. It is impossible to feel good if you are constantly looking down.

An upright posture, coupled with energetic movements, a bounce in your step, and a good smile, instantly give you an air of success, and what do these things cost you?

Absolutely nothing.

If you feel depressed, put on a smile, change your posture, and I guarantee that you will feel happier. Be proud. Walk like a peacock with its feathers spread out, not hunched over and looking down, as though life has defeated you.

Let's Summarize

If you speak quietly, with a slow and boring tone, and have a slouching posture, people won't think you are successful. As a result, you probably won't feel successful. So it is important to put the points discussed here into practice as soon as possible. Even if your financial position has not changed, you will start to feel better by putting these simple things into effect.

I don't know about you, but I like to deal with colorful people. By this, I mean people who are happy, smiling, and enthusiastic, both in their movements and voice tones. If I'm going to take on an employee, this is the type of person I want to hire. I don't want dull, boring, and depressing people who act as though they are made out of wood.

As I've already said, standing tall, smiling, and talking well are easy, and with practice they cost nothing. If you've ever talked to shop assistants and said to yourself, *they're not very helpful* or *they don't look happy*, consider that you too, at times, might give off the wrong impression.

Smiling is contagious. You smile at people, and in most cases they smile back. If you look grumpy, chances are you'll see grumpy expressions mirrored around you. Try it out and see what I mean.

You may have heard the phrase, "Fake it 'til you make it." I prefer to say, "Acting as IF." Act as if you already have what you want, and the chances are you'll get it. Life is a self-fulfilling prophecy. If you're confident and take small steps, you'll start getting what you want. It may not happen overnight, but you'll get there.

Listening

You have two ears and one mouth, which suggests you should spend twice as long listening than talking. Most people get it the wrong way round and talk far too much, but being a good listener will help you immensely, both in your personal and business life.

I've discovered many money-making ideas by listening to people. I regularly listen to talk radio, where people phone in and give their opinions and concerns. By listening I get a good idea of what people are interested in and concerned about. I then develop products to fill people's needs, based on what I've heard.

Most people like to talk about themselves, and a lot of people divulge trade secrets by talking too much. I've watched people mess up sales that were in the bag by overtalking. When I was in telephone selling, I would always get off the phone as soon as possible, once the client had said "Yes."

Being able to listen actively is a very valuable and profitable skill. I've met people who claimed to really enjoy my company and conversation, but I had only spoken a few words during our meeting. People really do like to talk about themselves, so let them, and you'll be very well liked.

On the point of listening, let people finish before you butt in or try and preempt what they are going to say. First, it's annoying to be interrupted, and second, you can do yourself a lot of damage by wrongly assuming what someone is going to say.

Think before you speak. I know from time to time we all say things that we live to regret, but if you remember to think twice and speak once, this will happen less often. The same goes for e-mails, text messages, and social network chat. It's easy to send a message, but nearly impossible to get it back. Think twice before clicking Send, and make sure your message isn't saying anything you might later regret.

Dressing for Success

I believe you should never judge people by the way they dress. However, most normal companies still believe if you wear a suit and tie you are successful, but if you wear jeans and sweat suits, you aren't worth doing business with.

You need to dress to suit the occasion and the people you are meeting, taking into account their age and business. If in doubt, go smarter, but mainly you should dress how you think the other person would *expect* you to look.

The Right Dress Code for Men

The classic business uniform for a man is still a good suit, with a plain white or pale-colored shirt and stylish, colorful tie. A good-quality pair of clean, comfortable leather shoes finishes this outfit. Avoid striped shirts, shirts with a different-colored collar to the body, and novelty or garish ties.

Grooming

You should have clean hair and be well shaved. If you have a beard or moustache, make sure it's clean and tidy. Aftershave is fine, but it should never be overpowering.

Good Skin

Most men spend little or no time looking after their skin, yet a good complexion is important. There are now many male grooming products, such as cleansers and moisturizers. Start including them in your daily routine, and if you get stuck on what to buy, ask your wife or girlfriend for help.

The Right Dress Code for Women

Although women have more options and can be a bit more adventurous with colors, I still think a good suit is the best bet. Dress smart, but not overly sexy, as this will intimidate both men and women.

Grooming

Hair should be neat and clean, and should not cover the eye or cause you to keep sweeping it away. Although coloring your hair is acceptable these days, you must ensure the color is well-maintained and professionally done.

Makeup

Makeup is an essential part of everyday life for most women. However, I believe more women should take advice, read books, or attend courses on how to apply makeup effectively to suit their face and skin. I also believe that, like clothes, makeup should be varied to suit the occasion.

Applying makeup well makes a big difference to the final effect, so if you're not sure how to do it, take a look on YouTube for makeup tips. Search for "pixiwoo," and you'll find an abundance of advice.

Perfumes

I don't believe there is a problem with perfume, but it must *not* be too overpowering. Remember that less is more.

Your Inner Voice

Outward appearance is important, but your inner voice is more so. The silent words we all say to ourselves produce feelings. These can be positive, happy, and life-enhancing, or negative, unhappy, and detrimental. Others will sense how we're feeling, and react to us accordingly.

Just as we need to project the right external voice, we also need to have the right internal voice. As you read this, do you hear a whiny, sleepy, apologetic voice, or a rich, strong, energetic voice?

If you have just read this paragraph sitting slouched in a chair, and your inner voice sounded sleepy and lacking in energy, try this. Read the previous paragraph, but sit back in your chair with your head up. Read the paragraph silently to yourself, in a strong, energetic voice. Feel excited about what you are learning. You should be excited—your life is changing for the better!

Happy Music Makes Happy People

Music and the sounds that surround us can have a massive effect on our mood. If you don't believe me, try listening to a morbid, slow song, then listen to a fast, upbeat song. It makes a difference, doesn't it?

Pay attention to what you're hearing, especially around bedtime, as this really can effect what's going on in your subconscious mind.

3

What Do You Want Out of Life?

UNLESS YOU KNOW WHAT YOU want to achieve, you'll never get it. Excuse me for being blunt, but the biggest reason for not living life to its fullest is not because you're unlucky, disadvantaged, bad at math, or whatever. It's because you've never sat down and laid out your goals and ambitions.

Imagine going into a travel agent and saying: "Send me somewhere." The agent would say, "Where do you want to visit?" You would say, "A really nice place, you know, a place I can be happy. A place I can have an important job, a beautiful wife, some nice kids. A really great place." Could a travel agent help you? Of course not. People can't help you until you tell them exactly what you want.

What *Do* You Want?

I suppose you want lots of money and a good life? That is not a specific goal. People say this all the time and then spend their money on the lottery. You have to be far more specific than this. Even if you believe in yourself, success is impossible without specific, well-defined goals.

I've asked hundreds of people: "What do you want out of life?" and very rarely do I ever get an answer. Even when I do, it's something like "I want to be happy." Most people just don't know what they want, and that's why they don't get anywhere.

19

Before you read this book, I would be amazed if you had already written a goals sheet. I would guess that 99 percent of the population don't have well-defined or written goals.

When I was younger, I didn't have any specific goals. I had ideas and vague generalities, but not any goals. As a result, I didn't get anywhere. Until I developed specific, well-defined goals, I did not succeed. When I wrote down my goals, everything changed for the better.

Your Road Map to Success

If you wanted to drive from London to Edinburgh, would you get in your car and drive in any direction? Or would you plan out a journey, get a map, and think about where you were going?

Most people are on the road to nowhere, unsure about where they're going, and sometimes even travelling in the wrong direction.

Until you map out your life, you will never achieve anything. You need to know what direction you are travelling in, why you are travelling in that direction, and what you are going to find along the way. Setting goals and mapping out your life is the foundation to success.

Now this may sound tedious and boring, but in fact it is very exciting. It's your chance to write down anything and everything you want out of your life, like writing a letter to Santa Claus. As long as you are good and take action to succeed, you are guaranteed to get everything on your wish list—and probably even more.

Where Will You Be in Five Years Time?

At this point, you probably can't answer this question. Chances are, you couldn't tell me where you will be by the end of this year. However, work through the next section, and you will soon have extremely precise and positive answers. By positive, I mean a can-do answer like "I will own my own business," rather than stating what you don't want, such as "I don't want to be on the scrap heap."

The following two charts are very important to your success.
Fill them out.

Don't pass them over and say, "I'll do that later" or "I don't need goals." I suggest you get a piece of paper, pen, and a ruler; copy out this chart in your own handwriting; and fill in the blanks.

Think hard about your answers. This is not a game.

Chart 1 Financial Needs

This chart is about what you need right now. Imagine I met you today with an open checkbook and offered to take care of all your immediate needs. List the things you need, such as:

Bills paid

Rent or mortgage paid

Home insurance

Clothing

Medical insurance

Car running costs

Food

Chart 2 Financial Wants

In this chart, you should list what you want in your life, from a financial/materialistic point of view. This list is very personal to you. After all, not everyone wants a Ferrari.

Suggestions

Rolls Royce/Ferrari F458/Porsche 911*

$900,000 House/Apartment in . . . *

One-year trip around the world

$500,000 in the bank

A gold Rolex watch

A Chanel suit

A certain piece of antique furniture/painting

To stay in the world's leading hotels

To eat at a top restaurant

To own a racehorse

*NOTE: Specific wants—state the actual location of your dream home, for instance, New York or London, and be as specific as you can. You might even name the street, such as townhouse on Baker Street, London. State the number of bedrooms, and extras such as tennis courts and swimming pools. Describe the house as if you already own it or are about to buy it today. If you want a car, state the model, color, and extras, such as Ferrari F458, with Alpine stereo and air conditioning.

Nonmonetary Goals

As well as financial goals, it's important to have nonmonetary goals. Achieving money alone is shallow and unrewarding. If you only have monetary goals, you'll never achieve true happiness or success.

This section of the book is about *you*, so it's a great place to start setting and achieving nonmonetary goals. By the end of this section, you'll be in the right frame of mind to achieve these personal goals. If you follow my advice during the rest of Part II, you will feel able to create your reality and overcome any obstacles you may face.

What are nonmonetary goals? Let me give you some examples:

Losing weight

Getting fitter

Improving your confidence

Finding a partner

Being more assertive

Learning to speak well

Nonmonetary Goal Assessment Sheet

A nonmonetary goal assessment sheet should be made for each aspect of yourself that you wish to improve. For example, one sheet for being more assertive, another for public speaking, and so on. Here is what your sheet should look like:

The personal goal I will achieve is _____.

I will benefit from this goal because _____.

The projected goal will be achieved by _____.

OBJECTIVE	ACTION STEPS	DATE ACHIEVED
1.		
2.		
3.		

REWARD
1.
2.
3.

Copy out the above sheet onto $8\frac{1}{2} \times 11$ paper, creating one sheet for each personal goal. I suggest you put your sheets in a ring binder and treat them as a diary, updating your progress until your goal has been achieved.

Notice how the goal sheet divides goals into three steps. It's easier to achieve lots of little tasks than one big one. You can add more steps if you wish, or take some steps away.

Rewards

After each step, you should reward yourself—giving yourself an extra-special reward when the final step is completed and the goal is achieved. Leaping from one goal to another without rewarding yourself is a bad idea. You'll find it hard to keep motivated, long term, if you don't reward yourself along the way. Rewards help us to keep going.

Many people who achieve success in business tend to miss out on holidays, or even short breaks, and this is a very big mistake. Taking time off allows your body and mind to recharge, see different sights, and come up with great ideas. Many of my best ideas came to me while relaxing on holiday. I came up with a very successful financial trading system, not in some boardroom or office, but by the Bellagio Hotel pool in Las Vegas.

Defining Nonmonetary Goals

Nonmonetary goals are sometimes intangible, and harder to recognize, so I've created something to help you.

The list below suggests qualities that you may or may not wish to have. Next to each quality are the numbers 1, 2, and 3.

If you already have the quality, circle the number 3 beside that quality. If you don't want the quality, circle number 2. If you don't have the quality, but *do* want it, circle number 1.

Qualities

To be more assertive 1 2 3

To be more friendly 1 2 3

The ability to finish what I start 1 2 3

To stop wasting time 1 2 3

To be a leader 1 2 3

To improve my relationship with my spouse 1 2 3

To be in good health 1 2 3

To be enthusiastic 1 2 3

To be admired by others 1 2 3

To organize ideas better 1 2 3

To feel less guilty 1 2 3

To be more considerate 1 2 3

To admit being wrong 1 2 3

To speak well 1 2 3

To be interested in others 1 2 3

To stop putting things off 1 2 3

To have a good sense of humor 1 2 3

To try new things 1 2 3

To face problems with courage 1 2 3

To avoid blaming others for my errors 1 2 3

To be ambitious 1 2 3

To take pride in my work 1 2 3

To have a good memory 1 2 3

Feel free to add anything else you wish to this list.

Once you have completed the above, you can add all the qualities circled "1" to your Nonmonetary Goals List.

Important Notes on Goals

1. The list of goals is for your use and benefit only. Be honest with yourself and don't write things down because you feel they will sound good if someone else reads them.
2. Make sure you really want the goal. When you write a goal down, you should feel passion and excitement. You will have to earn every item, and unless you really want it, you won't have the drive to work hard and get it. Ask for everything you truly want, but get ready to work hard.
3. Make sure your goals are positive. For example, "I want a $750,000 house," *not* "I want to get out of this awful studio flat."

    Always keep your mind fixed on the qualities and possessions you want, never on what you don't want.
4. Is the goal high enough? If you are currently earning $40,000 a year, don't set your goal to earn $50,000 or $60,000. Set it at $100,000. Challenge yourself. You may be afraid to write down a high goal for fear of falling, and that's understandable. However, what you strive for in life, you get. So you may as well reach for the peak of the mountain.
5. Make sure your goals are realistic, but don't limit yourself. If you want to earn $500,000 next year running your own business, that's fine. You've acknowledged that you need to work for your money. An unrealistic goal is to make $500,000 by gambling or winning the lottery.
6. Make sure your goals don't clash. If you want to live in a $900,000 house, your income needs to be at a level to support this. If you want to own a private jet, then you are going to need money for landing fees, fuel, and so on.
7. Your goals should be a base, not a maximum. When I was stock-broking, we were given sales allocations, such as placing 500,000 shares in ABC plc during the next seven days. We earned commission on these transactions, and if we sold more than our allocation, we would earn extra commissions.

    Many brokers would sell their allocation within the first three days, then sit back and relax. Others would do the opposite—they'd take their time at first, then place their allocation within the last two days. Either way, most met their target. However, very few exceeded this amount.

Because the target had been seen as a maximum, as well as a base, it capped people's ability to achieve even more. Remember that your goals are a minimum, and you can exceed them.

8. Set time limits to achieve your goals. Be realistic about what you genuinely feel you can achieve in a certain time frame, but be optimistic too. I've found that setting a time frame has helped me greatly. I'll give you an example. I recently challenged myself to buy a new, red Ferrari F458 with cash within six months, and found the time limit helped me achieve the goal much more easily.

Fine-Tune Your Goals List

Study and revise your list until it contains everything you want, both material and personal. Now, rewrite your Goal List in the current tense. Instead of "I would like a million-pound home," write: "I own a million-pound home." Essentially, you are now writing your goals as if you already have achieved them.

If you listed that you wanted self-confidence, the ability to follow through and finish what you start, more energy, and owning a private jet, then your list should state:

> I am self-confident. I enjoy meeting new challenges, and I follow through and finish what I start. It's the year 2020, and I own a private jet and have found my perfect partner. I have energy and determination.

Summary

If you used this section correctly, you should now have a list of goals, both material and personal, written as if you have already achieved them. Make sure they are full and specific goals.

How Is This List Going to Help Me?

When I asked you earlier what you wanted out of life, you probably couldn't answer the question specifically. When I asked where you would be in five years' time, you probably stumbled. Now you have a positive list of what you want to achieve, and a time frame in which to achieve it.

Later, I'll explain how to put these lists into action. For the moment, put your lists to one side and don't show them to anyone.

So Where Do We Go Now?

Remember I said near the start of the book, "A journey of a million miles begins with one step"? You have now walked many steps, and are well on your way to being more successful. As you progress, it will become clear how all these small steps fit together, and, like a jigsaw puzzle, all the pieces will soon fall into place.

4

How to Reprogram Your Mind for Success

IMAGINE YOUR BRAIN IS A computer memory stick. When you were born, it was blank. You didn't know anything at all. Everything had to be learned. As a child you were taught how to read and write, and how to know right from wrong.

Any new information you learned was stored in your brain, just like when information is written onto a memory stick. Every time a teacher or parent gave you a positive or negative comment, it was stored on your internal memory stick. The problem with the human brain is that it stores both positive and negative information, and there is no delete. Any negative comments stored as a child may still affect you today.

Here are some examples of negative comments teachers or parents may have said:

"You never do anything right."

"You're always so clumsy."

"You'll never learn anything."

"You're stupid."

"You'll never be as good/nice/clever as your brother/sister."

"You're always lying, making mistakes, getting it wrong."

Do any of these negative comments sound familiar? Negative comments like these are all stored on your personal memory stick, otherwise known as your subconscious mind. Comments, together with any negative childhood experiences, are all stored in our subconscious.

What these negative experiences and comments create is *fear*. Most of us are held back by fear, in one way or another. We're scared of having another negative experience or comment, so we don't try anything new.

The fear that comes from our childhood programming sits at the back of our minds, and hinders us. It stops us achieving our goals.

Let me give you an example.

Imagine you're back at school, and the teacher asks a question. You think you know the answer and put your hand up. Unfortunately, you answer incorrectly. The teacher says, "That's the silliest answer I've ever heard," and everyone in the class laughs at you. How do you feel about putting your hand up and answering another question? *Fearful*. You'll most likely feel scared of failure and embarrassment.

If you are told you're stupid hundreds of times as a child, you will believe it. This in turn gives you a negative self-image. You see, the subconscious mind is noncritical, which means it has no regard for logic or questioning. When you are young, the subconscious mind usually accepts everything as reality, because your conscious mind hasn't grown mature enough to question things. As a result, you become what you think you are as a child.

The Power of Your Subconscious Mind

Let me give you some examples of how powerful the mind is, in determining our reality.

If you were four years old and I told you the first six letters of the alphabet were B, N, D, G, L, Z, you would not doubt me.

There are many teenage girls who suffer from anorexia. They have convinced their minds that they are fat, even when in reality they are dangerously thin.

I was an overweight child. This came from watching my parents overeating and thinking this was normal. Overeating disorders are, in nearly all cases, mind-related.

The memory stick in your head has recorded all your childhood experiences and is still ruling your activities today.

We need to record over old negative messages with new positive suggestions. We will clean out all your past mistakes and negative feelings, and replace them with happy, positive, and constructive thoughts.

How?

If you've followed this book correctly, you should have a positive list of your goals. That's the list you're going to record onto the memory stick in your mind.

Just as the negative messages in your head held you back, the positive messages will push you forward. A positive mental attitude is the key to unlocking success, energy, goodness, creativity, and power.

Dwelling on past failures, negative experiences, problems, and shortcomings now has no place in your new life. You will no longer carry this unwanted, useless, heavy baggage around with you.

Declarations

You will now put your lists into action and start feeding them into your mind. Your lists should consist of all the material items you really want and all the personal qualities you might need to acquire them.

Morning Declarations   Every morning when you wake up, you must read your list of goals in their positive, accomplished format.

Read out loud if possible, and read with conviction, belief, and enthusiasm. You can say, "I am successful, I am successful, I am successful . . ." hundreds of times, but if you don't add enthusiasm and belief, it's not going to work.

As well as reading, you need to visualize your goals. See yourself driving the car or opening the door to your new house. If you have a fear that you need to overcome, such as going for a job interview, imagine you are in that situation and feeling calm and in control.

If you find that photos or brochures help you visualize, use them. Request a brochure for your dream car, or download sales pictures of homes you'd like to buy.

Let your mind enjoy these new positive thoughts.

Night-Time Declarations   Every night before you go to bed, read your goals again and visualize your success. I have found night-time declarations to be very positive, and I suggest you read your goals once with your eyes open, then again with your eyes closed—visualizing your goals and success.

Feeling relaxed helps a lot with this process, and relaxation recordings can help a great deal. You can download relaxing music or natural sounds, such as the ocean or rain, or buy these sounds on CDs. Remember to say your goals as if you have already accomplished them. "I own a million-dollar house." "I am brave and capable." And so on.

Now you may say, "I don't have my dream house. I'm living in a one-room apartment." Yes, this may be where you are today, but you're not going to be there forever. By programming your subconscious mind now, we are preparing you for the future. We are not lying to our subconscious mind. We are telling the truth, just a little earlier than in reality.

Every Day, in Every Way, I'm Getting Better and Better

Émile Coué was a nineteenth-century French psychologist and pharmacist who pioneered optimistic autosuggestion with his patients. One of the positive phrases he used to help patients was:

Every day, in every way, I'm getting better and better.

Notice that the phrase is positive and in the present tense. "I'm getting better," not "I will get better."

Before dispensing medicine to his patients, Coué would praise the formula and tell patients how well it would work. By instilling this belief in his patients, Coué discovered that the medicines worked much better.

Waking Up to a Bright Day

The fact that you have been fortunate enough to survive another day is a gift. Look out of the window and see sunshine, even if the weather is dull.

Every morning when you wake up, stretch your arms up and say "Yes! Today is a good day and it's getting better." Even if the day doesn't turn out to be your best, you started the day the right way, and, I assure you, your day turned out better than if you'd started it by saying, "Today is a bad day."

There's no such thing as "getting out on the wrong side of the bed." You choose whether you have a good day or a bad one. Is a sunny day good and a rainy day bad? It's all down to your perceptions and needs. There are certain parts of the world where a rainy day is a happy day, because water is needed for crops and animals.

Starting the Day the Right Way

As we've already mentioned, it's important to review your daily goals in the morning. It's also vital to have breakfast, as this helps set your body up for the day. Research shows that overweight people often skip breakfast. Eat breakfast like a king, lunch like a prince, and dinner like a pauper.

Feed your brain with positive information and your body with nutritious food in the morning, and you'll have energy and positive feelings for the day ahead. Allow time in the morning to review your goals and eat a good breakfast. If you don't have time right now, you'll need to get up earlier.

It's very easy to train yourself to wake up earlier. If you normally wake up at 7 A.M. and have to be out by 7:30 A.M., try waking at 6:50 A.M. for a week, 6:40 for the next week, and so on, until you have enough time for breakfast, reviewing your goals, and preparing for the day ahead.

Preparing the Night Before

Here's a tip I use when catching an early morning plane. I prepare everything the night before, laying out the clothes I need to wear, packing my tickets, passport, money and so on, and leaving the bags I need by the front door.

I also have a checklist of things I need to do before I leave the house, then tick off each point as it's done. I take the list with me when I leave, so if my mind asks, "Did I put the burglar alarm on?" I can check the list and put my mind at rest.

How to Turn a Seven-Day Week into an Eight-Day Week

If you woke up one hour earlier each day, you'd add seven hours to your week. That's almost one whole working day. Over a year, one hour less of sleep will give you an extra 365 hours. You can use this time to read, exercise, meet friends—whatever you want.

I'm not saying you should give up sleeping. We all need sleep. Our mind and body need repair time, but there is no excuse for over-sleeping. If you were to sleep for 15 hours a day, you would not become any more beautiful or intelligent than if you only slept for 8 hours a day.

Why Lie-Ins Are a Bad Idea

I know many people enjoy staying in bed until 11 A.M. on the weekends, but this is time wasted. Time is one of the rarest commodities we have. None of us is getting any younger, and once today is over, you can't bring it back.

I hate to sound morbid, but I can't guarantee how long you are going to live, and I certainly don't know if there's life after death.

Treasure your time. Jump out of bed every day and enjoy life. If you honestly think there is nothing better to do than oversleep, you need to add "take up fun hobbies" to your goal list.

A common reason for people oversleeping is that they don't want to get up. They feel life has dealt them a bad hand, and there is nothing worth getting up for. It's also a fact that people who don't enjoy their work tend to oversleep. Any parent knows that many children wake up at the crack of dawn on Saturday and Sunday, yet on a school day you have to drag them out of bed.

Some people sleep to try and forget and escape their problems. However, this is no long-term solution. Your problems will still be there when you wake up in the morning, until the day you take action and control of your life.

Margaret Thatcher, the great British prime minister and Iron Lady, claims to have slept no more than six hours a day.

At the age of 85, my Italian grandmother got up at 5 A.M. every day. By 8 A.M. she had cleaned the house, done the shopping, and made the day's dinner. She put many younger people to shame.

I know everyone is different, but it's been medically proven that very few people need more than eight hours' sleep. Imagine if I told you tomorrow would be the last day of your life. Would you lie in, or would you be wide awake, trying to get the most out of your last few hours?

Resist the temptation to sleep in at weekends. It really messes up your body clock and sleep patterns. Get up at the same time every day and you'll feel much better.

> *For the past 33 years, I have looked in the mirror every morning and asked myself: "If today were the last day of my life, would I want to do what I am about to do today?" And whenever the answer has been "No" for too many days in a row, I know I need to change something.*
>
> —Steve Jobs, *Apple*

Going to Bed Satisfied

As we've previously mentioned, your nighttime declarations are very important. Every night before you go to bed, read your goals and visualize your success. Reflect on the day, focus on the positive moments, and congratulate yourself on your good work. As for the negative factors, reflect on them and ask yourself what you have learned from the experience and what you can do differently next time.

Learn a New Piece of Information Every Day

When you go to bed and are in review mode, ask yourself what new piece of information you have learned today. If you haven't learned anything new, plan how you will tomorrow.

Summary to Setting Goals, Visualizing, and Your Subconscious Mind

I know some people will say, "What a load of rubbish and mumbo-jumbo" about the idea of setting positive goals and visualizing success. My answer to these people (which may include you at this stage) is "What do you have to lose?" Nothing, except a little time. But you have everything to gain. The advice given here has worked for me and thousands of others, so give it a chance, and you'll soon be seeing great results.

How Does Visualizing and Using Your Subconscious Mind Work?

Think about this question. Do you really need to know the answer? What really matters are the results. I assume you use an electronic calculator and believe the results it produces, but do you understand how the calculator works? I doubt it. Do you know how the Internet works or how an e-mail gets to you?

The many things I have visualized and fed into my subconscious mind have become reality, and yes—in the early days, I did think it could just be a coincidence. However, after a while there were too many coincidences. The things I had visualized turned into reality, almost exactly as I had visualized them or written them down.

Before I used positive thinking, I would worry about a problem or visualize something going wrong, and guess what? That's exactly what happened in real life.

Here is my nonscientific explanation of how goals and visualizing work. When visualizations come true, it's not because the fairies make them happen. It's because you take certain actions that lead to a programmed goal, even if you don't consciously know it.

Have you ever driven your car on a long journey and arrived at your destination, but you're not quite sure how you got there? This is your subconscious, running on autopilot and getting you where you need to go.

I recently read about Roger Bannister, the first man to run a mile in under four minutes. This had always been considered impossible, but Bannister's own self-belief made him able to try anyway. He claims he ran the race hundreds of times in his head before it happened in reality. Essentially, he trained his mind for success, and then the reality followed.

How People in Sports Train Their Minds

When you see great sports people win gold medals, you will be aware that they have spent days, months, and even years practicing their sport and building up their physical strength. However, did you know all champion sports people also practice mental exercises to build up their minds?

Some sports people even use spiritual chanting to drive positive feelings. Have you ever seen a weightlifter lifting a heavy weight? Notice how he makes noises as he lifts the weight. It is his mind that is giving him the extra strength.

Some years ago, there was a big uproar about how certain countries from the Far East were doing extremely well in the Olympics. These teams were breaking many records, and although everyone thought that they were on drugs or using special running shoes, it was concluded there was no wrongdoing. These athletes had, I believe, perfected the art of "mind over matter" to such a high level that the competition just couldn't compete.

I've already mentioned how the four-minute mile was run in the mind, hundreds of times before it was run in reality, but one of the most amazing acts of mind over matter happened in 1994, when George Foreman (better known by some of you for the George Foreman Grill) reclaimed the heavyweight boxing championship.

George was 46 years old when he won the championship—ancient in the world of boxing—and had been out of the ring for over 10 years. His opponent, Michael Moorer, was 26.

Before the fight, George didn't look in great shape, and there was no hiding his age. The odds were totally against him and big George was way behind on points, yet he won and knocked Moorer out in the tenth round. The clip can still be found on YouTube—search "Foreman Moorer"—it's a classic. I believe George's mind won him back the championship.

Never, never, underestimate the power of the mind. Positive mental attitude is one of the biggest factors that will help you lead a rich, healthy, and successful life. Start using it *today*. It's free, and extremely easy to tap in to.

We still know very little about the power of the mind, and scientists are just scratching the surface, but I honestly believe we all have amazing powers. With just a little fine-tuning, you can give yourself the winning edge.

On the subject of George Foreman, never let anyone tell you that you are too old. You are only as old as you feel, and age is certainly no reason to put anything off. People are living longer than ever, and the days of staying in the same job your whole life are gone.

At the age of 100, American funny man George Burns was asked about dying. He said, "I haven't got time to die. I'm booked."

So I Just Think About It, and It Happens?

No. Positive thinking without any action is like looking at a cookbook and expecting it to magically bake a cake. You need to DO SOMETHING.

The combination of positive thinking, goal making, visualizing, and taking action is an amazing formula for success. Use these powerful tools together, and you will become far more "lucky" and successful than you could ever have imagined.

Setting New Goals and Keeping the Momentum Going

After setting your goals and achieving them, you should be ready to add new ones. Life is a journey, and although there will be times when you'll want to stop and admire the view, the most rewarding and exciting times are when you're working towards a goal.

As you grow older and become more successful, you will think of bigger and better goals. There will always be new goals and adventures; people who think they've done everything in life are very much mistaken.

5

Making Decisions, Dealing with Problems, and Taking Action

AS MENTIONED EARLIER, EVERYTHING THAT happens, good or bad, comes from an action that we have previously taken. The decisions that you make (or in some cases, don't make) shape your life, both in the short term and long term.

In life you will be faced with many decisions, and your aim should be to make more right decisions than wrong ones. We must also realize that the right long-term decision will not always be easiest in the short term. There are times when you have to endure short-term pain for long-term gain.

How many times have you said, "If only I'd listened to" or "If only I'd left earlier" or "If only I'd invested in XYZ" or "I knew I should have"? It's frustrating to make the wrong decision, but here are some techniques to help you make the right ones.

The Ben Franklin Method

If you need to make a tough decision, take a piece of paper and write your dilemma at the top, phrased as a question. Draw a line down the middle and head one column "Benefits" and head the other column "Disadvantages."

Put your positive head on and write down all of the advantages underneath the benefits column. Then put your negative head on and write down the disadvantages.

Take your time and think hard. This exercise is for your benefit. Be honest with yourself and write down absolutely every benefit and disadvantage you can think of.

When you have finished, look at all the advantages and weigh them up against the disadvantages. Your decision is made for you. You can enhance the system by adding a value to each point such as Money = 8, losing contact with friends = 10.

Here's an example. Let's say you were offered a job in Germany. Here is how your decision sheet might look:

Should I take up the new job in Germany?

For

Better pay (8)

Better conditions (10)

Better opportunities for promotion (8)

Chance to make a fresh start (8)

Against

New unknown surroundings (7)

Losing contact with friends (10)

New language (7)

Total for = 34   Total against = 22

The Coin Method

Here is another way to help you make your mind up—tossing a coin, but with a difference. The difference is that it doesn't matter which way the coin lands.

Before you think I'm totally insane, let me explain. You have no doubt you have to make a decision, where deep down you know what you should do, but on the surface you aren't quite sure.

With a decision of this sort, take a coin and make heads yes and tails no. Here's the important part. When you toss the coin, which side are you really hoping for? What's your inside feeling? Say, for instance, that I was choosing whether to invest in a company. If I felt I didn't want to invest when I was tossing the coin, and heads came up, I would not invest even though the coin said yes to invest.

It's a great way of letting your true feelings out. Try it.

The Sleep-on-It Method

You must have heard people say "I need to sleep on it" before they make a decision. Here is a way to do it effectively. Before you go to bed, write down your question or problem. Tell yourself you need an answer by morning, then drift off to sleep thinking about your options.

The next day, ask yourself the question and see what comes into your mind. In most cases, you'll get a clear answer that points you in the right direction.

The Flow-Chart Method

This method uses logic to make a decision. You write down the question or problem, and then chart all the possible outcomes. It's easy and immediate, and helps explore all your options.

Once You Have Made Your Decision

After using one or maybe all of the above methods to make a decision, listen carefully to the answer you receive and respect it. This is especially true if the answer is "no," "don't do it," or words to that effect.

Sometimes it can be very hard to say no, especially in personal matters. Many people end up in unhappy or abusive relationships, yet they just can't say no and move on. I'll discuss personal relationships later in the book, but for now, just remember if the answer is no, and you truly know that's the right answer, make sure you act on this advice.

If the answer is yes to your decision, put all doubts and negative feelings to one side and *take action*. Remember, you have tried your best and thought out the decision carefully. You must do everything in your power to help that decision become the right one. If negative thoughts such as, "I'm not sure if I should have done this," come into your mind, then immediately block them out and remind yourself of all the positive things that made you make the decision.

Taking Action

Making a decision can be hard, but taking action and sticking with it is even harder. Unless you take action, your decision is worthless. Unless you make the call, write the letter, call a meeting, or whatever, then nothing will ever happen.

Once you have made your decision, put it into action as soon as possible. Taking action can be scary, and you may find your stomach churning and your mind working overtime. However, soon after you have taken action, you will feel better.

Whether it's a decision to resign, end an arrangement, move to a new country, announce you are an alcoholic, announce you are gay, start a new business, or take a trip around the world, when you make a well thought out decision and take action, good things happen.

Whatever the reaction to your action or announcement, stay true to your decision. Many people don't like change or sudden news, so you may find those close to you don't react well when you tell them. However, once they have got over the initial shock, everything will be much calmer and easier.

What Is Holding You Back from Taking Action?

The main thing that stops people taking action is *fear* of the unknown. For many people, it's easy and feels safer to do nothing. After all, taking action means the possibility of failure.

The questions you must ask yourself are, "What do I have to gain from taking this action?" and "What do I have to lose by not taking this action?"

If you have more to gain than lose, you *must* take action and go for it. If your current position is bad and possibly getting worse, then what do you have to lose? If you're near the bottom, then there's only one way to go, and that's up.

This is the only life you have. You must take opportunities, stick your neck out, take some risks, go against the flow, and—most importantly—take a stand and claim your piece of the pie.

Let me ask you a question. What would you do differently if you knew you could not fail?

How Never to Fail Again

I have the best system ever invented for beating failure. Never try anything. Stay in bed all day, don't take risks, don't take any opportunities, and, as long as your roof doesn't cave in, you should be okay.

Let's not kid ourselves. You will fail at one time or another. I've failed. Everyone's failed. When you see a famous and successful person, you see her success. What you probably won't see is all the failures behind that success.

When you watch a TV program or film, do you think it was all shot in one go, with no edits or mistakes? The truth is there were many mistakes, missed lines, retakes, and so on. The average film shoots about one hour of footage for every five minutes shown.

One of the smartest self-made businesswomen in this century and last has to be Madonna. You may not like her style, music, or films, but you must respect her perseverance and success. She doesn't ever give up. She makes a film, it flops, she starts again. She has written hundreds of songs. Many of them are successful, but not all of them. I recently watched a biography on Madonna which showed that even though she was broke and had not achieved any success, she acted as though she was already a superstar. In her mind she had already visualized what was going to happen. Madonna definitely knew what she wanted and did whatever she had to do to achieve her goals.

When the late actor Cary Grant was interviewed, he was asked how he went from a nobody to a world-recognized actor. His answer was "I started to act like the person I wanted to be, and eventually I became that person."

As stated earlier in the book, "acting as if" can make a big difference to your life. You can start "acting as if" right now. It will cost you nothing and will start opening new doors immediately. Many call this the law of attraction—like attracts like, and we get what we focus on.

While I am not advocating dishonesty, a BBC program called "The Real Hustle" is a great example of "acting as if." In the program, con artists demonstrate real-life scams, and nine times out of ten the scams work because the con artists "act as if." They become hotel managers, workmen, or officials, and instantly make others believe in them. On a lighter note, a film called *The Wedding Crashers* uses the same technique.

Dealing with Failure

We have all experienced failures in our life. No one is immune to making mistakes or wrong decisions. However, failures can be managed, and the negative effects can be reduced. In fact, most failures turn into the best lessons you could ever hope to receive, if you view them the right way.

Take Thomas Edison. While trying to build the light bulb, he was interviewed by a young reporter. The reporter asked, "Mr. Edison, how does it feel to have failed 10,000 times?"

Astonished and perplexed, Edison replied, "I have not failed 10,000 times. I have successfully found 10,000 ways that will not work and I am 10,000 times closer to finding a formula that will work."

So take note. Failure is all about perception. If you go for a job interview and the outcome isn't successful, this doesn't mean you have failed. You have successfully proven that you and the job weren't right for each other, so you can move on to the next one.

Failure is about learning. Mistakes are fine, as long as you learn from them and don't keep making them over and over.

As a matter of fact, people who make the most mistakes are usually the ones out there *doing something*. When I worked for a bank years ago, I made many mistakes and had quite a few queries on the transactions I handled. However, I soon realized I was doing more work than everyone else—around three deals to everyone else's one. When volume was taken into account, I was actually making fewer mistakes than everyone else.

If you don't do anything, you will make fewer mistakes. But you won't get anywhere. If you work hard and take chances, you'll make more mistakes, but you'll learn and achieve much more too.

Getting a Second Chance

People have short memories. In life, there are many second chances, and sometimes even a third or fourth chance. It's amazing how quickly people forgive and forget mistakes. If you don't believe me, think about this:

How do political parties get reelected after all the mess-ups they make? It's simple. As long as they can avoid making too many mistakes in the run-up to the election and make some good promises, they are home and dry. People will forget about all the scandals, tax increases, and spending cuts.

Here's another example. How many food scares can you remember? There have been scares about eggs, meat, diet soft drinks, food additives, pesticides, and many others. When a scare hits, sales drop, and people stop buying the product. The scare is all over the newspapers and on television, but after a few months sales come back because people have short memories.

If you mess something up, try again. Chances are people won't even remember your mistake in a few months. If you want a business loan and mess up the application interview, wait a little while and try again. The chances are, the person who turned you down has forgotten you and will be more than willing to hear why you deserve a business loan.

If you attend a job interview and are turned down for the position, you'll receive the standard rejection letter or e-mail. Most people forget all about the job at this point. However, why not phone the company back and explain why you really are the right person for the job? Ask for a second chance. They can only say no. Because most people don't do this, most companies will find your persistence impressive. They may well give you the benefit of the doubt and ask you back.

This tip can work if you are selling a product, asking for start-up capital, or making an offer on a house.

I recently read about a self-made millionaire, Dan Pena, who was turned down by nearly 200 different banks. He finally got the financing he needed and is now worth around $250 million.

Most people would have given up at being turned down 2 or 3 times, and definitely 50 times, but Dan didn't. He didn't let rejection put him off, and nor should you. It's just an opportunity to try harder.

On the subject of failures, did you know that Colonel Sanders, the Kentucky Fried Chicken inventor, was flat broke and 66 years old when he first tried to sell his chicken recipe? He was turned down by over 2,000 restaurants before finally getting his recipe accepted. Now there is a KFC on every main street.

Dealing with Rejection

Here is one rejection that I'm sure everyone reading this book has encountered—being turned down by someone you're attracted to. Being turned down might hurt today, but you'll get over it. If you never try to get together with someone you like, then you'll never get the date of your dreams. And anyway, a no today isn't a no forever. Tomorrow, it might be a yes.

Here's another point on the dating subject. There are many famous, rich, good-looking men and women who do not have partners and spend their nights alone. I believe this is because people don't ask them out as much, for fear of rejection.

If, in our opinion, someone is better looking or more successful than us, we instantly worry that we'll be rejected. But the truth is, it's amazing what can happen if you try. If you aim high and it doesn't work out, there's room to come down. Aim low, and you haven't really succeeded all that much. So aim high and deal with the rejection if and when it comes. You might be surprised when it doesn't.

Why You Don't Need Horoscopes, Tarot Cards, or Clairvoyants

I've noticed a disturbing trend lately. More and more people are looking for guidance, hope, and a miracle cure from horoscopes, tarot card readings, and clairvoyants.

What may appear a bit of fun can actually become addictive and a controlling factor in many people's lives. If you find yourself looking to these sources for guidance, it's time to start taking control of your life again.

Let's get real. It's *your* actions and decisions that shape your life and lead to success or failure. It can be tempting, in turbulent and restless times, to seek guidance from horoscopes and psychic readings.

However, on the whole you are wasting your time and money. Your goals and lifelong plan should be your inspiration.

Positive thinking and your own self-confidence are what will see you through good and bad times.

If you want to know what is going to happen in the future, then ask yourself. Visualize what you want to happen. Don't take advice from someone who doesn't really know you. The answer to your problem is not in the stars. It's inside you.

It's not healthy to live your life on the basis of someone else's suggestions. You should control your own future. As you become more successful, confident, and in control of your life, I guarantee you will never look at a horoscope column again.

Focusing on the Positive

By simply changing your focus, you can alter the outcome of an event. Let me give you an example.

Imagine you are driving a car and suddenly lose control. You are heading straight for a wall. Now, if you keep focusing on the wall, the chances are you are going to hit it. However, if you can focus on another object, you will steer towards that and reduce your chances of hitting the wall.

This may sound far-fetched, but ask any professional racing car driver and I guarantee they will know and use this technique.

If you put energy into focusing on a negative outcome, the chances are that's what you'll get.

Congratulations! You're a Loser

If you constantly focus on a negative outcome, you will become an expert at losing. Have you ever said:

"I knew I'd never find a parking space."

"I knew I wouldn't make a sale."

"I knew she'd say no."

You should not congratulate yourself for predicting a negative outcome. The chances are that you created that negative outcome yourself, when you could just have easily have created a positive outcome.

It's Harder Today to Be a Success

I often hear people say, "If only it was the 1980s or 1990s, I could have made money. There were more opportunities in those days." What a load of rubbish. If you were in the 1980s or 1990s, you would probably say, "Oh, if only it was the 1960s or 1970s."

The fact is, there is no better time to make money and seize opportunities than today. Negative losers console themselves with "back in the good old days," but the only people they are fooling is themselves. Even when economies are booming, there are still many companies that go broke, and when the world is deep in recession, there are plenty of companies that continue to do very well. I made most of my money during so-called recessions.

One day, I was standing in line at my bank, waiting to pay my checks in, when I overheard two businessmen talking about how bad business was, how the recession was terrible, and everything in the world was wrong. There I was, 20 years old at the time, paying in thousands of pounds with a big smile on my face. They could have been doing the same thing if they'd stopped blaming the world for their problems and taken control of their lives.

Some of the world's biggest companies, including IBM, GE, and FedEx, were founded in recessions or depressions. Life is what you make it. Don't buy into the doom and gloom headlines.

The Hot Dog Seller

This story is about a man who once sold hot dogs by the roadside.

He was illiterate, so he never read newspapers.

He was hard of hearing, so he never listened to the radio.

His eyes were weak, so he never watched television.

But enthusiastically, he sold lots of tasty hot dogs at a fair price.

His sales and profit went up.

He ordered more and more raw material and buns, and sold more hot dogs.

He recruited a few more supporting staff to serve more customers.

He started offering home deliveries. Eventually he got himself a bigger and better stove.

As his business grew, his son, who had recently graduated from college, joined his father.

Then something strange happened.

The son asked, "Dad, aren't you aware of the great recession that is coming our way?"

The father replied, "No, tell me about it."

The son said, "The international situation is terrible. The domestic situation is even worse. We should be prepared for the coming bad times."

The man thought that since his son had been to college, read the papers, listened to the radio, and watched TV, he ought to know, and his advice should not be taken lightly.

So the next day, the father cut down his raw material order and buns, reduced his staff, removed all the special schemes he was offering to customers, and was no longer as enthusiastic.

Very soon, fewer and fewer people bothered to stop at his hot dog stand, and his sales fell rapidly.

The father said to his son, "Son, you were right. We are in the middle of a recession and crisis. I'm glad you warned me ahead of time."

The moral of the story? Make up your own mind. Recessions can be self-fulfilling. Sometimes it's better to ignore bad news.

Beating Yourself Up Has No Positive Effect

When something goes wrong, you make a mistake, or an outcome is not as expected, how do you deal with it?

I used to mentally beat myself up, and ended up feeling bad. I now know there is no positive advantage to beating myself up, even if I'm to blame for a bad situation. It only makes me feel terrible, which in turn makes things worse. Yes, you should accept responsibility for your life, but at the same time you need to forgive yourself and move on.

Let me give you an example. Say you were reversing your car out of the garage and you hit something and dented your car. You could curse and tell yourself you should have been more careful, but would this make the dent miraculously fix itself? No.

If you spill coffee over your computer keyboard, feeling bad won't clear up the mess.

I've now learned to get over mistakes as quickly as possible and focus straight away on sorting the mess out and moving on. And you should, too.

Your Success File

A success file is personal to you, very simple to make, and can have a huge effect on your life. For everyone, there will be times when things seem to be going wrong. You receive bad news, and you generally feel you are fighting a losing battle. This is where your success file comes in.

What Is a Success File?

It's simply somewhere you store all your positive documents, photos, certificates, music, and anything else you are proud of and/or that makes you feel good. It can be a shoe box or an actual file—it's completely up to you.

Perhaps you don't feel like you've achieved anything. Well, I don't believe you. Everyone has some success in their life, even if it was winning the egg and spoon race at school.

Dig deep. You could choose school reports, medals, trophies, certificates of achievement, or copies of any licenses you hold. (If you have a driving license, this is an achievement in itself, as you've passed your driving test.)

You can also include happy photographs, a cartoon strip you like, a picture of your favorite film/pop star, autographs, a book of your favorite jokes/quotes, a newspaper clipping, or tickets from a sports game where your team won.

If all else fails, copy out parts from this book that make you feel good. There are some—I hope!

Don't put anything in the file or box that makes you feel nostalgic or sad. A photo of an ex-partner isn't a great idea. Nor is a photo of the dream car you once owned, but had to sell.

The idea of this file/box is to help you through any troubled times by showing you what you have achieved and making you feel happy. It's a way to distract you from any current problems and help you realize you are a *winner*.

It's all too easy to brush away past successes and remember only the current problems. Your success file will help you remember when things went really well, and give you hope that they will again.

I don't recommend that after every little problem you rush for the file. You should be strong enough to get through minor things. The success file/box is for emergencies only. You may not ever need to use it. In fact, your aim is to add even more contents to your success file, not refer to it constantly.

Your Worst Enemy and Your Best Friend

I'D LIKE TO INTRODUCE YOU to two people you've known all of your life. They are your worst enemy and your best friend. Who are they? *You.* These two people live inside your head. They're with you every day, 24 hours a day, and will be with you for the rest of your life. You may think the opinions of your friends and family count, but they are nothing compared to the two people you spend all day with.

You need to make sure your best friend is much bigger and stronger than your worst enemy. Your worst enemy will never die. He or she will always be there, ready to come and see you, especially if you are going through a low point. However, if you help your best friend develop and grow, you will find he or she becomes your companion much more of the time, and you'll hear from your worst enemy less often.

Developing Your Best Friend

Your best friend wants you to be happy. He or she likes it when you get something right, achieve success, or learn new information. Your best friend likes to hear positive thoughts, stories, and music. Your best friend also likes to smile and laugh out loud when you do.

To keep your best friend strong, you need to treat him or her well, and in return you will see this friend more often. Your best friend knows that things don't always go right, but also that any problem, challenge, or setback is only temporary and can be overcome.

You must feed and water your best friend. Give your best friend happy music, positive thoughts, and joyful stories.

Getting Rid of Your Worst Enemy

Your worst enemy likes to see you suffer. He or she laughs when you make a mistake or things go wrong. He or she likes drugs, alcohol, cigarettes, and other nasty habits. Your worst enemy likes sad somber music and violent or sad films. Your worst enemy doesn't like laughing and hates seeing you try to achieve anything. Your worst enemy is out of shape and does not believe in reading books and furthering education.

You must starve your worst enemy, so that he or she shrinks and goes away. There is no place for your worst enemy in your life.

Do I not destroy my enemies, when I make them my friends?
—Abraham Lincoln

Summary

You may think this is all a little crazy. You may believe you don't have a best friend and worst enemy living inside your head. Okay, then. Who do you think your inner voice is? When you read a book or think of something, who does that voice inside your head belong to? You decide whether it is your friend or enemy. It's much better having an inner voice that says, "Yes we can" than "Don't be silly—every time you try something, you fail."

Your expectations open or close the doors of your supply. If you expect grand things, and work honestly for them, they will come to you. Your supply will correspond with your expectation. There is no medicine like hope, no incentive so great, and no tonic so powerful as expectation of something better tomorrow.

—Orison Swett Marden

Learning to Love Yourself

Unless you can learn to be at ease with your own mind and body, success is going to be a very, very steep hill to climb.

Most of us are unhappy with something about ourselves. Either we are too short, too tall, too fat, too thin, have a big nose, big ears, or big hands. Even so-called supermodels are unhappy with parts of their body. As well as physical features, many of us feel unhappy about our mental abilities, too. These bad feelings hold us back. So how can we overcome our insecurity, fears, and failings?

First, write them down. List what you don't like about yourself, and then analyze what you can do about it. Be totally objective. Are your ears really that big? (By the way, I read that people with big ears live longer.)

Once you've openly analyzed the list, cross off everything you can't do anything about. Physically crossing out items with a pen will help mentally remove them from your mind. In this electronic age, there is still merit to pen and paper.

As for the remaining shortcomings, what can you do about them? For physical problems like weight, you can take action. If being overweight is making you unhappy and insecure, you must do something about it (I'll talk more about diet and exercise later).

As for height, I believe people who think they are too short can increase their height through exercise and improving their posture, as already mentioned.

In this day and age, some parts of our body can be improved by plastic surgery. There is a price for this, however—both in money and physical suffering—and you may find yourself no happier after the procedure.

It's quite common for people to feel obsessively unhappy with another part of their body following plastic surgery. Many people spend thousands of pounds on surgery, only to find themselves in a cycle of finding fault with their body. Once people have cosmetic surgery, they often want more surgery, until they've had the whole menu!

Just like everything in life, the *mind* is really where it all starts. It's all about perception. If you're looking for fault in your body, you'll find it.

I believe cosmetic surgery does have its place, especially for rectifying birth defects, major skin problems, or scarring after an accident. However, if you want cosmetic surgery for vanity reasons, there is usually a deeper problem inside, which means most likely the problem is in your mind.

You should believe in your own body and mind. When you start thinking more positively, through positive mental programming, you'll find many of your shortcomings can be eliminated, simply by thinking them away.

Other shortcomings can be overcome by attending training courses or changing your lifestyle. For example, shyness can be helped a great deal by public-speaking classes. A healthy lifestyle and good eating can help weight and posture problems. For general wellbeing, associating yourself with winners and other positively programmed people will help you immensely.

Many insecurities and inadequacies are manufactured by companies trying to sell you something. I'm sure you've seen TV ads presenting a problem and then offering a solution.

Stop Worrying Today

My life used to be negatively affected by worrying. I was a master at it. If there was a degree in worrying, I should have taken it—I would have passed with flying colors. I don't know why I worried so much, as it certainly didn't make life any better. However, over the years I've learned to reduce my worrying by proving to myself, time after time, that what I worry about never happens. I haven't stopped worrying completely, but I have learned to channel my energy into taking care of legitimate problems, rather than worrying about anything and everything.

Here are some things many of us worry about:

1. Things That Are Unlikely to Happen
   Worrying about things that will probably never happen makes you feel bad and wears you down. I used to put a lot of energy into worrying about unlikely occurrences, but I learned worrying is like visualizing failure instead of success. When I started putting my energy into visualizing success instead, my life changed for the better.

2. Things That Have Already Happened

Worrying about things that have already happened is a pointless exercise. It won't change the outcome and doesn't make you feel better. I used to carry negative thoughts over to the next day, but now I close off yesterday's worry and start every day afresh.

3. Worrying about Health Problems That Aren't Real

I used to wake up in the middle of the night and convince myself I was dying. Even though there was no evidence that I was terminally ill, I'd worry just the same. Sometimes I'd read articles about illness, and then be convinced I had that illness. Now, thanks to positive mental programming and a healthy diet, I don't worry about any health problems that aren't real.

4. Worries Created by People Selling Products

I used to be a sucker for advertising. If I received a sales letter telling me I could be at risk of XYZ, and I should buy a certain product, I'd worry. Many ads are written to play on our worries, and they're very effective. The key is to remember that the worry has been created to sell you something. Remind yourself that you never had that worry until someone told you to have it.

5. Legitimate Worries

Legitimate worries are where our efforts should be placed. Normally, legitimate worries are only about 5 to 10 percent of all worries. A legitimate worry is something you can take action to solve. For example, if you've planned an outdoor wedding tomorrow and you're worried about the weather, you can take action by having tents on standby.

Perhaps you're flying abroad tomorrow, and are worried you won't make the flight on time. Plan out your trip to the airport, leaving plenty of leeway in case anything goes wrong, and you'll feel much better.

Positive action will help you overcome legitimate worries. If you can't take positive action, then your worry isn't legitimate.

Tips to Help You Deal with Worries

1. Define Your Worry

Think clearly about what your worry really is, and if it helps, write it down.

2. Ask Yourself How You Can Remove or Reduce the Worry

If there is nothing you can do, stop worrying. Kill the worry with positive thoughts.

3. If You Can Remove or Reduce the Worry, Write an Action Plan

You may never need to use your action plan, but knowing it's there will help you stop worrying.

4. Ask yourself, *Is There a Way to Eliminate the Worry?*

Many worries can be eliminated entirely, with a little positive thinking and planning. Let's take the example of the outdoor wedding. Is there any way to change the wedding venue and hold it indoors? If there is, you can remove the problem and remove the worry.

Why Worry?

Some words of wisdom for you . . .

There is only ever one thing worth worrying about: Are you well or are you sick?

If you are well, then you have nothing to worry about.

If you are sick, you'll either get well or die.

If you get well, there is nothing to worry about.

If you die, you'll either go to heaven or hell.

If you go to heaven, there is nothing to worry about.

If you go to hell, you will be so busy shaking hands with friends, you will not have time to worry.

I don't know who wrote the above, but I thought it was worth including in the book. Hopefully it put a smile on your face.

Summary on Worrying

Concentrate on legitimate worries. Throw all other worries out of your mind. Use positive thoughts to blast the worries out of your head. You don't have time to carry them around. I speak from experience. Worrying about things that might never happen made me ill and stopped me getting on with my life and achieving success.

Is worrying holding you back? If it is, try programming your mind with a daily declaration such as, "I am in control of my life and I don't have any worries."

Finally, I thought that you'd be interested to know the results of a survey, which asked people about their fears and worries. Here are the top 10 answers:

1. Public speaking (people are terrified about speaking in front of a group)
2. Heights
3. Insects and bugs
4. Financial problems
5. Deep water
6. Sickness and ill health
7. Death (I personally thought this would be higher up on the list)
8. Flying
9. Loneliness
10. Dogs

With the exception of number seven, we can do something about all the above fears. A fear of public speaking can be overcome with practice, and many of the other fears can be dealt with by hypnosis.

In order to succeed, your desire for success should be greater than your fear of failure. I don't know the key to success, but the key to failure is trying to please everybody.

—Bill Cosby

The Past Is History; the Future Is Where to Look

Change is the law of life. Those who look only to the past or present are certain to miss the future.

—John F. Kennedy

Past failures, including traumatic relationships and public embarrassment, seem to be the biggest factor stopping people moving on and getting ahead.

I don't want to sound uncaring, and I understand people suffer from very painful divorces, loss of loved ones, and business failure. However, the past is one thing that this book can't help you with. What has already happened is history.

This book will help you look to the future, and see hope and happiness in the brighter things ahead.

Many people dwell on ifs and whys, but wallowing and torturing yourself over the past has no positive effect. Channel your energies and focus on the future, because you can do something about tomorrow, but you can't do anything about yesterday.

Instead of running towards our dreams, we are often running away from a fear of failure or a fear of criticism.

—Eric Wright

7

Magic Words or Tragic Words?

THE OLD SAYING, "STICKS AND stones will break my bones, but words will never hurt me" is a little misleading. Words have amazing powers, both positive and negative. Words, both in written form and spoken form, can change the way we feel and act.

Words can make us laugh, cry, and cooperate. They can also cause hurt feelings, anger, and irritation.

Spoken words have extra power, as there is the added factor of emotion and tone of voice.

Our mind is talking all day. You have around 50,000 thoughts each day, all delivered by your inner voice. If you ensure that most of your thoughts are positive, you will give yourself a big advantage in life and will feel charged up from within.

When it comes to talking out loud, you've probably also heard the saying, "If you can't say anything nice, don't say anything at all." Very true, and a saying I'd advise you to live by.

When I worked for a big company, the rumor mill worked overtime. People gossiped, started rumors, and generally bad-mouthed each other. They'd tell me about Joe down the corridor, and so on, but I would stay out of any gossip. Those who talk about others behind their backs will talk about you, too. That's a fact.

Don't get involved in these types of conversation. Rise above them, and I guarantee you will gain more respect. In today's electronic age, this also applies to e-mails, chat rooms, and Facebook. Think twice before posting any message you may later regret. Posting anonymously isn't a good idea, either—these days, people can be traced very easily.

Tragic Phrases

Some words are for losers, not winners like you. I want you to say goodbye to phrases like these:

"I know I'm going to miss the bus." (Say that and I'm sure you will.)

"It's not my day today." (Keep telling yourself that and *yes*, you'll have a bad day.)

"I wish I was still in bed." (There are millions of sick people who would gladly swap your life for their deathbed.)

"I'm scared of computers." (I've never been beaten up or hit by a computer.)

"I can't understand . . ." (It could be that you don't want to understand.)

"He's always picking on me."

"I knew this was a bad idea."

Words to Erase from Your Life

Doom, low self-esteem, pessimism, defeat, gloom, misery, negativism, anger, failure, malice, bitterness, ignorance, anxiety, hatred, and losing.

You'll see a lot of these words in newspapers. Why? Because unfortunately bad news sells better than good news, so much of the media around you are focused on negative stories and words.

Magic Phrases

"Today is a good day, and it's getting better."

"I am excited, and I look forward to this new challenge."

"I can fix this problem."

"There's a better way to do this."

"I will do whatever it takes to be successful."

"Past mistakes and failings are history. Future successes and achievements are present."

Words to Add to Your Life

Positive, energetic, valuable, sharp, bright, praised, brilliant, excellent, dazzling, astounding, appreciated, winner, dynamic, resilient, intelligent, success, achiever, happy, and exciting.

Start using these words more in your everyday vocabulary, both when speaking aloud and internally. Learn one new positive word each day.

On the subject of learning, if you can learn just two new words a day in a foreign language, within a year you'll have a fairly good vocabulary.

I can accept failure. Everyone fails at something. But I can't accept not trying.

—Michael Jordan

Listening to Skeptics

The cynic knows the price of everything and the value of nothing.
—Oscar Wilde

I often hear things like, "You don't want to do that, you want to do this"; "That will never work"; "I think you should . . ."; and "Somebody has already done that."

Skeptics are all around us. They look for the flaws in a scheme, and don't believe in anything they don't understand. Even when you show them hard evidence, they still convince themselves they are right and everyone else is wrong. In one of my businesses, I showed genuine commission checks people had earned acting as agents for my company. These checks ranged from $2,000 to $50,000. In my literature, I showed copies of the checks and an extract from my bank statement, showing that the checks had been cleared.

One gentleman just could not believe people could earn these amounts, even in the face of concrete evidence. Because he didn't earn that much, he didn't believe anyone else could.

I'm not saying you should be an unrealistic optimist. We live in turbulent times, and regrettably everyone isn't as honest and truthful as they should be. However, being a complete skeptic means you'll never try anything, and consequently won't succeed.

Can You Give Away Free Money?

Over the years, various experiments have been carried out, whereby passersby are offered free money. Hardly anyone ever takes the money, as it's far too great a stretch for our rational minds to believe that free money would be handed out. It's fine to be rational, but it's also important to keep an open mind. If you don't, you may well miss great opportunities.

Taking Advice

Let's say you've decided to start your own business. You've done your research and are very excited about the project. Because you are so excited, you decide to tell your friends, family, and anyone else who will listen. You present your case and say: "What do you think?" Here is where the problems start.

The chances are that however nice your friends and family are, they are also negatively programmed. Few people buy books like this one, and in most cases have no experience of business.

When you ask for an opinion or advice, you need to qualify the person who is giving the advice. Let's say your friend John's reply is:

"I don't know if that will catch on." You need to ask John to explain his answer fully—and here are the key questions to ask: "Have you ever run your own business, John?" and "Do you know about this area of business, John?"

If John is working at minimum wage in a factory that has nothing to do with your proposed area of business, I wouldn't take much notice of his answer, whether positive or negative. If John is running his own successful business, preferably in a similar field, then I would listen.

You can save a lot of trouble and money by accepting informed and objective advice. It may hurt in the short term, but can save heartache, time, and money in the long run.

A point on getting advice from the Internet. I see many people willing to share a lot of personal information openly on the Internet, as well as seeking advice from complete strangers. While the Internet can be a good way to do market research, be careful about believing what an unknown person says in a chat room.

How I Give Advice

If someone asks me for advice, I always think carefully before answering—especially if I'm making negative observations. I know from personal experience how people can put doubts in your mind, which can lead to abandoning projects that could have been successful.

When I was thirteen, I made money while the other kids were out playing. I wrote a computer game and got into buying and selling computer software. I made around £200, which was a lot of money for a 13-year-old back then, especially since everyone else was earning peanuts doing paper routes. I knew there was more money to be made if I had more capital, but at 13 it was hard to get anyone to take me seriously.

I told my father about the venture and asked for assistance, but he shot the whole business down. Totally demoralized, I dumped the project. Please don't let anyone do the same to you.

If a good friend asks for advice, think hard before you give it. I believe many great ideas have been abandoned because of advice based not on any facts, but fear.

When I give advice, I listen carefully to the proposal and, in most cases, won't give an instant opinion. Instead, I'll do some research and fact finding. I'll only give an opinion if I genuinely feel I can offer useful, well-informed advice. If I can't give good advice, I will say so.

In the past, people have approached me about entering my line of business. Even though they were technically talking about going into competition with me, I still gave them objective and truthful advice. Some people took the advice and stayed out, but others gave it a try without heeding my warnings, and failed miserably.

Professional Advice

Professional advice can sometimes be worse than no advice at all. Again, I speak from experience.

There are thousands of lawyers, bankers, and accountants who offer bad advice. When people take on a professional adviser, they think this releases them from their obligations and they don't have to worry about anything. *Get real.* If you take on an accountant, and there is a problem with your tax return, do you think the accountant will get into trouble? I don't think so. In the UK, if your limited company accounts are filed late, it's *you* who gets fined.

If you receive bad legal advice, it's *you* who'll suffer the consequences. Unless you want to find another solicitor to sue your previous solicitor, that is!

Professional advisors are human, and they make mistakes—just like you. They have bad days, they have matrimonial problems, they have health problems, and they have financial problems. (Yes, bank managers and accountants have bills and debts, too!)

Professional advice should be taken with caution. However, you will need expert help at times, and when you do, make sure you research and ask the right questions when looking for your advisor.

Never give an adviser 100 percent control of anything. An advisor should be able to prove herself and be happy to let trust build up over time.

If you ever say anything along the lines of, "I'm now in your capable hands and I'll leave it with you," you're heading for trouble.

Remember, your advisor works for you, not the other way around. Whatever advice they give, the final decision is yours. No solicitor can make you plead guilty if you want to plead innocent. It's you who'll end up in jail if it all goes wrong.

So to summarize, listen to family, friends, and professional advisors, but qualify whoever is giving you the advice and make up your own mind.

Taking Responsibility for Your Life

When I ask people what they want out of life, a common answer is, "I want to be happy." When I ask them to define happiness, in most cases they can't.

Happiness is a state of mind, and is personal to everybody. However, in many cases we let our happiness be defined by advertising agencies who are trying to sell us something. Although most ads don't directly say "This will make you happy," that's really what they're suggesting. Most ads are there to persuade you that a product will make you happy, either by making you sexy, look good, or feel great.

How are cars sold? Not by showing traffic jams, accidents, or being pulled over for speeding. No—car ads are all open roads, beautiful women, and handsome men.

What one person calls a happy place, someone else will call hell. Some people think living in a penthouse apartment in London or Manhattan is happiness. Others think living on a farm in the middle of nowhere is happiness. Some people think the ideal holiday is sunbathing on an unspoiled desert island. Others think it's shopping in New York. Personally, I've had some great holidays in Las Vegas, but many people hate the place.

Think about actual things that make you really happy, and be honest. Don't say lots of money, as money alone isn't happiness. In fact, on the subject of money, what is it, really? Just pieces of paper, or a plastic card settled by numbers in a bank account. Money itself isn't very exciting, unless you are into collecting bank notes. It's what money represents that's exciting, and what you plan to exchange it for.

How to Make Yourself Happy at Any Time

The easiest way to make yourself feel happy right away is to change your focus and think of a time when you *were* happy. Even if you've had a rough life like me, there have been times in the past when you've been happy. Remember this time in as much detail as you can. Remember how you felt, and remember what you saw and heard.

I've used this technique many times to help me out of tough spots. With some practice, you can call up the good times and focus on the positive, not the negative. Give it a try.

Accepting Praise and Taking Criticism

Many people today are quick to criticize or complain. However, they're not so quick to praise or compliment. In this online age, it's very easy to give feedback or write a review. People are quick to write a poor review, yet few take the time to give good feedback when they receive good service or are happy with their purchase.

Some people look to God or go to church when things go wrong. They pray for forgiveness and ask for help. However, how often do these people ever give thanks for happiness, health, and prosperity? Very rarely, if ever.

I try, wherever possible, to thank people for a good service and pay them sincere compliments. I was recently on an airline, and the cabin crew were excellent. On leaving the aircraft, I made sure I thanked them and told them what a good job they did.

Accepting Criticism

Nobody is perfect, least of all me. I'm always in search of self-improvement, and criticism is one way we can all self-improve. If someone says I've done something wrong, or am failing in some area, I take notice.

If the criticism is well-founded, I take action to rectify or improve the matter. However, if the criticism is unjustified, I don't take any action and try to put the negative thought out of my mind.

You know, deep down, if a criticism is justified or not.

If a criticism is justified, it's pointless to get defensive and deny the truth. It's also pointless to apologize, but do nothing to rectify the problem.

If someone makes a justified criticism, take action and solve or eliminate the problem.

It's very fashionable right now for companies to ask their customers, "Are we providing a good service, or have we messed up?" This is all well and good, as long as these companies actually listen to the customers and take action. After all, for every one customer who complains, there may be a hundred more who don't say a word.

Some years ago, I made a complaint to a very big airline, advising them of a problem. I didn't receive an acknowledgement of the complaint, and when I travelled again using this airline they still hadn't fixed the problem.

Summary

You should give praise when it's due, and accept praise when it's due. Don't shrug off a compliment with, "Oh, it's nothing." You're robbing yourself of praise. Accept praise, and let it sink in to your subconscious mind. It's good for you.

As for criticism, if it's valid, accept it and act. If it's not, reject it.

To avoid criticism say nothing, do nothing, be nothing.

—Aristotle

Asking Questions Makes You More Successful

As children, we learned by asking questions. Listen to a child, and hear how many times he or she ask questions, or says, "Why?"

When we become adults, we ask fewer questions—perhaps because we feel people will think we're stupid if we don't know something.

I believe the brightest children are the ones who ask the most questions. As long as their teachers or parents take time to answer, children will be very smart and beat the averages.

As an adult, we should continue asking questions. We should ask questions such as, "Is there a better route?" or "Can I do this a better way?"

If you work in a sales environment, you should already know that if people ask a valid question, they are interested buyers.

We should ask our partners or loved ones questions too. I know it may be embarrassing, but all the top lovemaking therapists say that asking your partner questions leads to better lovemaking.

We should ask our customers questions. For example, "Do you prefer black or red?" or "Which day do you prefer to shop on?"

Many new products are developed by asking questions, or by answering the "why" statement. Take, for example, the Polaroid instant camera. You take your picture, and it pops out the bottom of the camera. Within a minute, you can see it.

I read that the Polaroid camera was invented as a result of a child's "Why?" question. After having her photo taken by a normal camera, the child wanted to see the photo right away. She couldn't understand why she had to wait for the film to be processed (which all films had to be, before digital cameras came along).

An inventor heard this "Why?" question, and sat down to work on the Polaroid instant camera—which, of course, went on to be a massive seller.

Summary

Asking questions is a good way to learn, and taking notice of "Why?" is very important. Both in business and on a personal level, asking questions helps us find out if we are getting things right.

> *When you stop learning, stop listening, stop looking and asking questions, always new questions, then it is time to die.*
> —Lillian Smith

8

Associate with Eagles, not Turkeys

IF EACH OF US HIRES people who are smaller than we are, we shall become a company of dwarfs. But if each of us hires people who are bigger than we are, we shall become a company of giants.

David Ogilvy

I know people who look down at others, but will never look up to someone who is doing better than they are. They like to think they have the best house or car on the street. Well, they may have, but if they go a mile down the road, their house and car would be the worst.

If you always look down instead of up, you will never progress. Focus downwards and the chances are you'll start moving downwards. Aim high, look up, and notice people who are doing better than you. This will help you soar like an eagle, not run around like a turkey.

Find yourself a role model—someone you can relate to. Try to associate with people who are positive and winning at life. The people you surround yourself with can help you or hold you back. Now I'm not saying you should always be chasing the bigger and better deal, but realize your true potential.

Let me give you an example of good association and bad association.

A good association is Weight Watchers. If you are trying to lose weight on your own, it can be very difficult. Weight Watchers brings people interested in losing weight together. The group encourages, sets goals, and has past slimmers as role models. Most people who visit Weight Watchers find the meetings very uplifting and get motivation and inspiration from them.

A bad association is negative people and downmarket pubs and clubs. You will find that very few people offer positive aspirations in a downmarket pub or club. The chances are that smoking, drinking, and drugs will be all around you. Add in a negatively minded fellow patron, and you're on the way down. However positive you are, if you spend enough time around depressing people, it is hard to stay positive.

I've been out with depressing people who believed that life was terrible and everything was bad, and after a few hours I started to feel quite down, even though I was very happy before I met them.

On the other hand, I've met happy, positive people who were interesting and really making something of their lives. When I meet these sorts of people, I want time to stand still. They inspire me, and I don't want to leave their company.

You must have heard the saying, "Birds of a feather flock together." Who are you flocking with? Negative, deadbeat people, or positive, upbeat people?

These days, you can flock together online too, so be careful which Internet forums and chat rooms you involve yourself with regularly.

It is better to be alone than in bad company.

—George Washington

Summary

Success breeds success. Learn about people who are doing well, and ask yourself how you can do the same. Associate with people who are trying to solve the same problem you have, such as losing weight, giving up alcohol, or learning to speak in public, and you will find support and ideas. You owe it to yourself to push as hard as you can and to maximize your true potential. Success is a journey, and travelling should be just as fun as arriving. Make sure you travel in good company!

A word of warning about good and bad associations. In life, there are hangers on and people who will use you. Don't associate with these people, and don't become one yourself either. A good friend gives as much as he or she takes.

Do you have any so-called friends or associates who only get in touch when they need a favor or a shoulder to cry on? Then read on.

A good friendship and relationship is based on give and take. It's not on taking more than you give. We all ask friends for assistance sometimes, but friendships should never be abused. If you take something today, make sure you give something back in the near future—and the same should apply to your friends. Any friend who is always taking isn't really a friend.

Dealing with Envy and Jealousy

Imagine I park my new Ferrari in front of your car. I step out and am wearing an expensive suit. I have a Rolex watch on my wrist and generally look happy and successful. What will be your first thought?

Some people might think, *Lucky so and so—wish I had a Ferrari.* Others might think, *He must be a drug dealer.* Or, *He probably won the lottery.*

These thoughts are envious and jealous, and don't get anyone anywhere. Envy and jealousy are signs of a loser mentality, so if you're experiencing these feelings, you need to take control of them right now.

Don't be angry or jealous of people who are doing better than you. Admire them, congratulate them, find out their secrets, and copy them. (As long as they're not really drug dealers!) Success is a wonderful thing. It can give you a map of how you yourself can be successful. So don't envy it. Emulate it.

I love to see successful people. Why? Because they are rare and I can learn something from them. They prove that success is achievable, which is good news for everyone.

One day, you could become far more successful than me. You may appear on TV or write a book. In fact, you may already be richer than me, but I don't envy you—I admire you, and I want you to do well.

This book is about making every reader more successful. Nothing makes me happier than hearing success stories, and if I have contributed a little to that success with this book—even better.

Working Smarter, not Harder

This phrase has a nice ring to it, but I believe if you work smarter *and* harder, you will reach the top much quicker. I'm not going to turn this into a science lesson, but let me explain the meaning of leverage, to show you how to work smarter and harder.

Imagine you have 20 heavy boxes to move. You could work hard, picking them up individually, or get a cart and push them along. It would be much easier to move the boxes using a cart, wouldn't it? And if you work harder to move the cart quickly, you could be done in no time.

Do you have a problem where leverage could help? Perhaps a repetitive job, such as monitoring the news, that you could have a computer do for you? Check out Google Alerts, and you'll see how your computer can save you hours of research time.

Of course you should work hard in life, but hard work alone will get you nowhere. I've met people who've worked hard for 25 years or more. They've started early and finished late, yet are still earning much less than many of those around them.

Results count, not the fact you've put in 10 hours a day for 25 years. A few simple changes can easily turn hard work into great results. Think of a farmer, using a horse and plough. Give the farmer a tractor and he'll triple his productivity, and have more time to market his products. Where in your life can you work smarter and make yourself more productive?

Learning to Adapt and Changing Direction

Many people are set in their ways and do the same things over and over again. There are new discoveries and inventions every day—many of which can make our lives easier—but if we don't learn about them or use them, we hold ourselves back.

Here is an example.

You drive to work every day, using the same roads. One day, you learn a new road has opened that will cut your journey time by 15 minutes. All you need to do is turn right a few miles on, instead of your usual left turn.

Will you turn right or left? The chances are, you'll take the normal left turn, because that's what has been programmed in your mind over many repeated journeys.

The only way to learn the new route is by sticking a note on the dashboard and thinking hard about your journey. After a few weeks of pushing yourself to take the new route, it becomes natural and automatic.

It can be hard to change things that are well programmed in our minds. But if you learn to break old habits and try better ones, you'll see much more success in your life.

Let me give you another example. If you had to see a surgeon for a heart operation, who would you want to be treated by—someone who qualified 50 years ago and has never done any further studying, or a younger doctor who's kept up to date with the latest medical technology and regularly reads medical journals and attends seminars?

I'm sure, like me, you'd prefer the second surgeon.

People always fear change. People feared electricity when it was invented, didn't they? People feared coal, they feared gas-powered engines. . . . There will always be ignorance, and ignorance leads to fear. But with time, people will come to accept their silicon masters.

—Bill Gates

Working Around Problems

Earlier on, I mentioned people who work hard but get nowhere. These people are a lot like flies, banging their heads against a window. I'm sure you've seen flies doing this—they want to get out the window, but they just don't understand glass!

This is what many people do every day. They hit themselves against the glass over and over again. The smart way to overcome the problem is to take a step back and assess what's really going on. Is there a way to do things differently? Can you go around the problem?

Here's an interesting saying, which I'm sure you've heard: "Some people are so busy chopping wood, they don't have time to sharpen their axes!"

Very true. By taking a few moments to examine a situation (and work out that you need to sharpen your axe), you can make your hard work more effective (and chop much more wood).

If you are out walking and there is an obstruction in your path, you wouldn't keep hitting yourself against it. You'd step back and walk around it. This is a piece of common sense you should apply in everyday life.

9

Personal Relationships

THEY SAY BEHIND EVERY GREAT man is a great woman, and vice versa. There is a lot of truth in this. A positive partner can be an inspiration, whereas a negative partner, who does not share your goals and aspirations, can be your worst enemy. Your decision to better your life, increase your income, increase your knowledge, or improve your appearance, may not be shared by your partner—and here we have a problem.

How can you tell if your partner is on your side? There is no simple answer to this question. But let me ask you this. How does your partner react when you suggest something new—a change, a new business idea, further education, and so on?

Does your partner always react in a negative and lethargic way, or sit up, take note, and give you constructive input?

If your partner is genuinely enthusiastic about your plans, your achievements, your goals, and your success, then you have a partner who will help you get to the top.

If your partner isn't enthusiastic about your striving for success, then you have a problem that will only increase as you become more successful and wealthy.

In a relationship, when one partner increases his or her income, changes the circle of friends, or gets into shape, a negatively minded partner may feel inferior or insecure.

These days, it's just as common for a man to be jealous of his successful female partner—and perhaps more so, because many men resent women being more successful than they are. Perhaps it has something to do with our caveman heritage, and men bringing back the food.

Which of these three categories does your partner fall into?

1. One hundred percent supportive, providing objective views and backing your ideas, visions, and goals. Ready to share your journey, trust your judgment, and help you all the way.
2. Average. Not particularly supportive, but not overly negative either. With some coaxing they agree to help you, but their heart isn't really in it. They think your goals and ambitions are okay, but doubt you will ever reach them.
3. Not supportive at all. Any suggestions or new ideas are shot down immediately and faults are found. They are quick to remind you of your past mistakes and that it is your fault both of your lives are a mess. They are very set in their ways, and would never consider moving away and losing close contact with their family and friends.

Which is your partner? One hundred percent behind you, or lagging? Deep down inside, you know the answer.

How to Help a Lagging Partner

Talk to your partner at length about what you're aiming to achieve right now, and why you're changing your life. You might even want to give them a copy of this book!

If, after a discussion, your partner is willing to make changes, then great. The theory is, if one partner starts leading a richer life, the other partner can easily copy.

Encourage your partner to try any new activities you're taking part in. If you're increasing your fitness and have joined a health club, bring your partner with you.

A lagging partner may need a kick-start, but once they understand the benefits, they will often be happy to follow you.

What if My Partner Still Lags Behind?

If you've tried hard enough to get your partner motivated and taking more interest in life, and you still find you're not getting any support, a *major decision* must be made. Negativity can drain you and hold you back.

Before we go any further, it may be wise to read my section on "Balance," and ask yourself if you're being fair to your partner. It's hard to expect his support if you are totally neglecting him.

If you conclude that your partner won't change, then your major decision is this: Will you give up your goals, ambitions, and future success, or be selfish and part company?

Having a negative partner can be worse than no partner at all. Trying to achieve success with someone negative draining your energy is like trying to run on a sticky surface. You just get nowhere, and tire yourself out trying.

Summary on Partners

Most partners are supportive of success, because, after all, if you start earning more money or getting invited to nice places, the chances are your partner is going to benefit.

Although an average partner is not as good as a 100 percent supportive partner, you'll probably still be able to persuade this sort of partner that change can be good.

If your partner falls way below average and offers no support at all, then radical action is required. You need to help improve your partner's self-esteem, and offer the techniques you've learned and adopted from this book.

If you have genuinely tried everything possible and your partner is still miserable (which in turn will make you miserable), the right solution is to move on.

Finding the Right Partner

It seems that dating is becoming more and more complicated in our busy, high-tech society. However, it doesn't have to be this way. If you have a good idea of what you're looking for, finding the right partner can be very simple.

What are you looking for in a partner? This is where you have to be 100 percent open and honest with yourself.

Don't take any notice of what anyone else thinks, or what magazines or Internet sites tell you. It's your life, and if you're looking for a lifelong partner, you must be happy with your decision.

Sometimes, family politics get in the way of relationships ("You can't go out with him because he's Jewish," or "They're a bad family").

You can't live your life for other people. *Do what you want.* Define the ideal partner for *you.*

I suggest you take a piece of paper. On one half write *me*, and on the other half write *my perfect partner.* Write down all your likes, interests, and qualities under *me.*

Now think about qualities you really want in your partner. Here is an example of what your sheet might look like.

ME	MY PERFECT PARTNER
Generous	Supportive
Enjoy traveling	Caring
Hard worker	Hard worker
Ambitious	Ambitious
Good sense of humor	Good sense of humor

Perhaps you think you want a supermodel, a multimillionaire, or a prince who lives in a castle, but are superficial qualities like these going to fulfill you for a lifetime? Sure—it might be exciting in the short term, but just like eating your favorite food every day, shallow desires can get old.

Look at some of the high-profile Hollywood divorces. A couple may be rich and beautiful, but if basic compatibilities aren't there, it will be a short-term and shallow relationship.

A note about your prospective partner. You may not find every quality you have listed in a partner, but if you can find most of them, you're on the right track.

You don't necessarily want your partner to be an exact mirror of yourself, either. It's good if your partner has some different qualities and interests to bring to the partnership.

Defining your ideal partner will help you find him or her. If you wander around not knowing what you want, you will never find the ideal partner because you don't know who you're really looking for. There are thousands of people out there saying, "I just can't find Mr. or Mrs. Right," but when you ask them to define Mr. or Mrs. Right, they can't.

Meeting Your Ideal Partner

If you sit indoors every night, hoping the right partner will knock on your door, you'll be waiting a long time. In life, you have to make opportunities. You have to look in the right places, which means avoiding downmarket pubs and nightclubs.

Take part in new activities. Join an evening class or go on a course. If you like travelling, go away on your own—you'll be amazed how many people you'll meet. Sure, it can feel lonely and scary at first, but it's a great way to shake you out of your comfort zone and give you courage.

If you really don't feel up to finding new activities or travelling alone, consider joining a dating agency.

Online Dating Agencies

You're probably thinking, *I'm not joining one of those. They're for losers who haven't been able to find a partner.*

Let me tell you something. Dating agencies have changed a great deal in the past decade. There are now many quality agencies that deal with successful, intelligent, fun people.

Many people these days run their own businesses and work long hours. This makes it difficult to meet a partner, but it doesn't mean that person is unattractive or desperate. There are some extremely rich and attractive people registered with dating agencies.

Joining an agency doesn't mean there's anything wrong with you, or that you're a failure. Far from it. Using a dating agency can be a very effective way for successful people to find partners.

A good online dating agency will take your personal information and partner requirements, and match them to prospective dates.

Although a computer is not guaranteed to find you an ideal partner, it can at least help to lay a foundation of common interests.

Don't think of dating websites as an instant way to find your dream partner. Instead, think of them as a starting point for expanding your friends and contacts—which in turn may find you a partner.

Upmarket Dinner Parties

These have become quite popular recently, and are advertised in quality magazines and Saturday newspapers in the personal sections.

If you're not willing to go to a dating agency, these might be a softer option. These dinner parties are designed to bring professional and affluent people together in a social atmosphere. Even if you don't find your ideal partner, you'll have a nice evening out, and you may make a few friends or contacts.

It's far easier to start a conversation and friendship in this type of environment than venturing to a pub or nightclub alone.

An old friend of mine attends dating dinner parties, and although he hasn't found his ideal partner yet, he's having a great time and meeting many new and interesting people. It also works like a pyramid, as the people you meet may invite you to another party with their friends, and so on. If you search the Internet for "dinner dates" or "singles dinner parties," you will find plenty of options.

Summary

Not everyone wants a long-term partner. Some men and women find they are happier and more productive living a single life. Many people now live alone, and find that as long as they have family and friends, they don't need a long-term partner. Life can be full enough without one. As I mentioned before, you're better off with no partner than a bad partner.

If, however, you feel life without a long-term partner is empty, take action and create opportunities to meet your perfect match. Don't stop until you've found your partner, and don't be ashamed to use introduction agencies and to seek guidance from others.

Act Before the Pain, Not After

Many people wait until something disastrous happens before they take positive action. How many of us rush to the dentist because we're in pain—a pain that could have been prevented by having regular check-ups?

Pain makes you act. However, prevention is better than cure. Despite the fact most of us know this, we often still wait for the pain and hope there is a cure.

Waiting for pain before you act is no way to run a successful life. Learn to identify problems early—preferably before they happen—and take action to *prevent*, rather than wait until you're forced to find a cure.

The fact that most people wait until pain before they act should tell you something useful, if you're thinking of setting up a new business. Where possible, choose a *cure* business, rather than a *prevention* business. You'll make much more money.

Let me explain. How many people take vitamins or medicine to prevent a cold? A few. But millions more buy cold cures. A lot more is spent on cure than prevention.

But back to you. In life, it's important to notice early warning signs. These could relate to health, personal life, or business.

I've made a fortune investing and trading stocks and commodities, and much of my success came from spotting early warning signs that told me companies and markets were changing.

I see many businesses ignoring early warning signs. Minor employee theft, bad security, computer passwords being written on pieces of paper and stuck on computer monitors, confidential paperwork thrown away without being shredded . . . these sorts of things are warnings that action needs to be taken. Early warning signs might sound insignificant, but they can blow up into problems if you don't take action.

Although I strongly believe in prevention, please don't confuse prevention with paranoia or constant worrying. Look out for early warning signs, but don't try and prevent anything and everything. If your home is in the middle of nowhere and there has never been a terrorist bombing in the area, it would be foolish to insure against acts of terrorism.

10

Getting It Done Now

WHEN YOU SEE AN EARLY warning sign, act quickly. Don't put off taking action. The simplest tool for getting things done is a to-do list. Write down your daily or weekly tasks, and don't stop until they're done.

Putting things off is one of the main reasons why some people don't get anywhere. Be someone who takes action. You can waste your time thinking of a hundred reasons why not to do something, but a far better use of energy is to work out how you *can* do it.

A winner will find ways to get things done. A loser will find ways to put things off. I have come across people who put more effort into working out why they can't do something than it would have taken to get the thing done. What a waste of energy!

Here are some of the common excuses people give for not getting something done:

1. Lack of Time

This is probably the most common excuse given for not taking action. And it's not true. You can find time for anything, if you have the will. It amazes me how people find the time to watch their favorite TV program, yet somehow have no time to fix the leaking faucet or mow the lawn.

People also spend hours on social sites like Facebook and Twitter. Are these really the most productive use of your time?

81

2. Feeling Overwhelmed

Some people have good intentions, but try to do lots at once and end up doing nothing. They write long daily to-do lists that can never be completed in one day, and end up feeling overwhelmed. The key is to break large tasks into smaller chunks. It's like eating a steak. Try to stuff the whole thing in your mouth, and you'll struggle, but cut it up, and it's delicious.

Make realistic to-do lists, and deal with one task at a time. Break big tasks into sections, and spread tasks over a number of days or weeks if necessary. Deal only with one task at a time, and don't look at your to-do list until that task is finished.

3. Not Wanting to Do It

There are times in life when you'll have to do something you don't want to do. If something has to be done, putting it off will not make the task go away. The quicker you get it done, the less time you'll have to think about it. Do the worst jobs first, and leave the best jobs until last. That way, you have something to look forward to.

As you become more successful, you'll be able to appoint others to do the tasks you don't particularly like. I don't like bookkeeping. It's repetitive, and I feel I can use my time and talents better elsewhere, so these days I pay a bookkeeper and use the time I gain to make more money at the things I'm good at.

4. It's Not Due Yet

It's amazing how quickly due dates come around. Why not do it now? You'll have it over and done with, and when the due date comes, you will be ready. In fact, why not score a few extra points and hand in the work early? Being one step ahead is never a bad thing, especially as unexpected tasks and time constraints crop up often in business.

5. I Just Can't Concentrate

Constant distractions make tasks harder to finish. Your job is to either work around or eliminate these distractions. If your office is noisy, come in early or stay late when it is quieter. E-mail, Facebook, and Skype can all be terrible distractions, and I advise logging out of these services when you're working, so they won't distract you.

Use whatever it takes to get the job done. When I worked in stockbroking, I was on a dealing floor with over 150 other dealers, screaming and yelling on the telephone. Often, I would take the phone and sit underneath my desk, so that I had some sound proofing. This helped me hear myself and my client, and improved my concentration.

6. If I Put It Off, the Task Might Go Away

There may be a one in a thousand chance that this could happen. Your boss might suddenly quit, meaning you don't have to complete the research project you've been asked to do. Someone else might notice your task needs doing, and pick up the slack. But you can't live your life this way. It's gambling, and a gambler is never in control of his or her life. Take charge and get it done.

7. I Work Best Under Pressure

This is an interesting reason, and although it's true for some people, I don't believe working like this all the time is good for the body or mind. If you prefer to work under pressure, then set yourself a strict time to have something done by—but make this time ahead of schedule. Fool yourself into thinking you have less time, and get the task done early. Should any unforeseen circumstances arise, you'll have time to spare.

8. I Need a Cigarette or a Stiff Drink First

This excuse normally crops up before an unpleasant task, such as firing people. If you must have a cigarette or stiff drink (and neither habit contributes to a successful life), deliver the news or do the task first, and then reward yourself afterwards.

9. It's Too Late Today

This is a classic, used by lazy salespeople—especially on a Friday afternoon. I've done some excellent deals out of normal business hours. If you are selling a product and all the other salespeople stop at 5 P.M., you'll have no competition after that time. You'll also find that receptionists and secretaries go home at 5 P.M., meaning it's more likely you'll speak to the boss directly.

10. It's Too Early

Starting early means getting lots done before anyone else. In terms of making sales calls, once again it means you'll have little competition, and directors often come in early, before their secretaries arrive. I've clinched many deals early in the morning, whereas, if I'd called later, the customer would have been elsewhere. As they say, the early bird catches the worm.

11. It Might Not Work

You will only find out if you try—and remember, starting with a negative outlook reduces your chances of success. Ask yourself, *What have I really got to lose if it doesn't work?* Probably just a little pride, and with positive thinking, you can get that back in no time.

12. I Keep Forgetting

I'm sure! If I had been meaning to write your paycheck, but I kept forgetting, you would no doubt remind me. If you genuinely keep forgetting something, write notes or ask people to remind you.

The chances are, you're forgetting because deep down you don't want to do the task. You don't tend to forget things you want to do.

13. I Don't Know How to Do it

This is not a legitimate reason to put something off. Seek advice, read the manual, call a technical help line, and do whatever you need to learn how to do it. It's amazing how many tasks seem complicated or boring from the outside, but turn out to be simple and enjoyable.

14. If I Do It Now, They'll Just Give Me Something Else to Do

I met someone recently who gave this excuse, and after a brief discussion it became clear he hated his job and was just coasting by. So if you use this excuse often, perhaps it's time to change jobs. You're not helping your employer or yourself by working somewhere you hate.

15. I'll Wait Until . . .

I've found that, without fail, there is no time like the present. If you have genuinely decided to do something, then start *today*. Life isn't a game. The sooner you start something, the sooner you'll see results.

Improve Your Memory

A good memory is an asset, and an essential part of success. A good memory helps us obtain qualifications, popularity (remembering people's names is very impressive), remember speeches, and generally improve almost all other areas of our lives.

Before I go any further, how do you rate your memory?

Excellent. I remember everything. In fact, I'm thinking of applying for Mastermind.

Average. I remember most things.

Poor. What was the question again?

Let's put a myth to rest. Most healthy people have very good memories. Our brains are sophisticated computers that can remember amazing amounts if used correctly.

How to Improve Your Memory Instantly

Stop saying you have a bad memory. If you rated your memory as less than excellent, your negative thoughts will create this reality. We have already discussed our subconscious mind, and that what we repeatedly suggest to ourselves becomes reality.

To improve your memory, use positive thinking and suggest to yourself repeatedly that your memory is excellent and improving every day.

Exercise Your Memory

I believe that the mind and, in turn, the memory is like a muscle. Unless you exercise it regularly, it will go rusty. Exercise your memory, and it will improve. Here's how.

Next time you go shopping, make a list. Study it and then put it in your pocket. Now go shopping without referring to the list. Trust your memory. As you approach the check-out, check the list and see how well you did. Keep up this memory-building exercise, and eventually you won't even need a list.

A good tip for this exercise is to imagine yourself buying the shopping beforehand. For example, if you have onions and potatoes on your shopping list, imagine you're at the supermarket and picking them up.

You Will Remember

Don't use qualifiers like "try to," "should," or "hope to." You WILL remember. Use bold, positive language like this, and you'll be amazed at the results.

Repetition

Repetition is still one of the best ways to learn and remember. Repeating information out loud has more effect than doing so in your head. You should *think* about what you're repeating, rather than just saying things, parrot fashion. Repeat things at short, regular intervals, rather than all in one session.

Remembering by Association

This technique is used extensively by waiters, casino card counters, and others who have to constantly recall information for a living. Here's how it works.

Link up new information with something or someone you already know. So, if you need to remember an onion, you can link this with your bank manager. Link a potato to your Uncle Ted, and a tomato with your sister, and so on.

When you want to recall information, think of the familiar name/person, then think again, and the new information should float into your mind.

Having a great memory will help you succeed in life, and with a little practice you may even become the next international memory champion!

You can use your memory for all sorts of things, but one of the most useful is to remember people's names and facts about their lives. In business, it's very impressive to be able to say to someone you only met once, "Yes, I remember you, Mr. Smith. How did the trade show in Germany go?"

Balance

One of the biggest problems we all face is living a balanced life. If you imagine a seesaw, too much weight on one side will make the other side go up, and vice versa. That's what life is like. Spend too much time at work, and your personal life and health suffers. Spend too much time at home, and work suffers.

I can honestly say that true success came to me when I was able to balance work, finances, health, and personal life. Only you know if you're neglecting your personal life or health. I certainly neglected my health at times, but now that I've corrected this imbalance the rewards are amazing.

For most of us, work and finances pose the biggest problems when it comes to achieving balance. Many people spend longer at work than anywhere else. In the "Making Money" section of this book, I'm going to tell you how to make plenty of money, but also spend lots of time with family and friends.

You *can* make more money than you're earning now, *and* have more time for your personal life and health. In fact, making time for health, family, and friends is vital for work and financial success. I believe that a balanced life creates the right state for success in all areas.

Trying to make money when your relationships are suffering and your health is poor will always be difficult, and this book aims to show you the *easiest* way to achieve success.

Let's look at what makes up a balanced life.

Your Mental Health

This book will help improve your mental and emotional well-being. With your goals outlined, increased self-confidence, and the use of positive thinking, your mind will be in excellent health. Keep following the advice outlined in this book, and this part of your life will be extremely well-balanced.

Your Physical Health

A balanced life includes good diet, exercise, and avoiding negative items like tobacco, alcohol, and drugs. We'll talk more about physical health in the next section.

Personal Relationships

A happy relationship with your significant other and children (if applicable) ensures you start the day on the right note. Making time for family and friends should not be a chore. It should be enjoyable.

Money cannot replace missed family time. If you have young children and they grow up never seeing you, you are letting them and yourself down. You will find that children who don't see their parents tend to have very little respect for them as they grow older. Make time for your children and significant other. You can't expect to gain respect and trust in a relationship if you're always at the office.

Take a genuine interest in your partner. If you find your partner is unsupportive, lethargic, or uninspired, think about what happens when you spend time together. Do you often unload all your problems and never listen to what's happening in their life? Relationships are 50-50, so if things aren't going well, think about the 50 percent you're responsible for.

Marital Disputes and Affairs

I believe most problems and affairs start because of neglect. The wife/husband feels the other partner has lost interest in them, and rebel by finding someone else. Some men/women have affairs for months, if not years, and the other partner still doesn't notice. There's no way this can happen if you're spending enough time with your partner and taking an interest in their life.

Many people say, "I'd love to spend time with my wife/children," and "I'd love to have a regular workout at the gym," but insist they don't have the time because they have to work and make money.

I understand that people need money to support their families, but be honest here—could you not make a few hours a week for the gym, or to spend time with your children and wife? No doubt you make time to watch TV, spend time unproductively on the Internet, and go out with your friends after work!

Summary

I've had my life in and out of balance, and I've learned it only takes a few simple steps to balance your life. Until your life is balanced, you cannot truly say you are successful. A balanced life will make you happier. When you can keep your personal, mental, and physical health in good order, you will find that the work and financial side of life becomes easier.

11

Food and Exercise

YOU MAY THINK, WHAT HAS exercise and food got to do with making money and becoming successful? Well, I can tell you from experience that eating the right foods and exercising regularly helps you become more successful.

Let me share with you some discoveries I've made.

I've spent a lot of my life overweight. I never used to exercise regularly, and was so engrossed in making money that I didn't think about diet. However, when I made the decision to change my eating habits and start exercising regularly, my life changed for the better, and I became more successful.

Although I'd been successful in business and able to keep my mind fit and positive, I neglected my body for many years. I now realize that keeping fit and watching your weight is an important part of success. Health is something we should all take notice of.

Why Being Fit Makes You Successful

When I lost weight, I instantly had more energy. Being thinner made me more confident and assertive, and generally more cheerful. This in turn made me feel good, and I became more successful as a result. You must have heard the slogan, LOOK GOOD, FEEL GREAT. It's true.

Like it or not, we live in an image-conscious society, and people judge you by your weight.

I also found that working out on a regular basis helped me reduce fatigue. Contrary to what you might think, exercise actually builds up your energy levels. It may tire you out while you're doing it, but you'll have much more energy afterwards.

Do You Suffer from Fatigue or Lethargy?

There are several reasons for feeling fatigued or lethargic, and all of them are physical. Let me discuss briefly the main causes of tiredness.

Diet

I will discuss overeating in greater depth in a moment, but as far as tiredness goes, the actual foods you eat are important. Certain foods give us more energy and help our minds work better. Others cause us to slow down and feel sleepy. A big lunch will, in most cases, kill your productivity for the rest of the day.

Cigarette Smoke

I am not here to pass judgment on smokers. However, medical research shows that smoking kills your energy level. Nicotine is a vasoconstrictor, causing the blood vessels to narrow, which means less blood reaches the brain. The blood that reaches your brain has more carbon monoxide, causing low energy and some drowsiness. The next time someone says that a cigarette helps him concentrate, tell him to do some research.

You don't have to be a smoker to be affected by cigarette smoke. Passive smoking is just as bad, if not worse. The smoking ban has helped make more environments smoke free, but if you have any friends who smoke at home, it might be best to avoid visiting them.

Lack of Exercise

Many people with desk-based jobs just don't get enough exercise. Humans were not designed to sit in front of a computer for eight hours a day. By simply standing up for a few minutes each hour, stretching or moving around, you will find fatigue can be reduced. Try standing up when you are on the phone, instead of sitting slouched in a chair. If you get a lunch break, go for a walk in the fresh air.

Most people have mobile phones and laptops these days, so how about working in a location where you can move around more? Much of this book was written in a variety of interesting locations.

Air Quality

Most offices have poor air quality, even the ones with air conditioning. I've found that an ionizer can help improve the air. It has a cleaning, calming effect, giving the air the same feeling as after a thunderstorm. Some ionizers can be used with essential oils that stimulate and invigorate you. If your company doesn't have an ionizer, buy a small, personal one. If you suffer from allergies or have breathing problems, you will notice a big difference by using one.

An Easy Way to Instantly Improve Your Health

Any ladies who want better-looking skin should definitely read this.

Most men and women *do not drink enough water*.

By water, I don't mean tea, coffee, soft drinks, or beer. I mean straight mineral or filtered water, preferably not sparkling.

Water seems to be a neglected cure for many problems, including fatigue, dark and puffy eyes, kidney problems, bad skin, and much more.

Experts vary in their recommendations on daily water intake, but around two to three liters is the general wisdom. I always push myself to drink at least six to eight large glasses of water a day. It is possible to overdose on water, but very unlikely. Drinking around three liters will certainly not do you any harm.

I'm not going to turn this book into a health and fitness guide, as there are many good books on exercise and healthy eating. However, what I will say is *do* think about what you eat and start a regular exercise routine. From my experience, it is better to exercise for a shorter period every day or every other day, than exercise for four hours all at once.

You Are What You Eat

Most diets don't work. In fact, people usually regain all the weight they lose on a diet within one or two years, and gain extra weight on top. They would have been better off if they'd just maintained their original weight!

My Personal Mind Diet

If you are lucky enough to be in good shape and at a comfortable weight, you can skip this section. However, if you're looking to lose weight and, most importantly, keep it off, read on.

Overeating is nearly always in the mind. Yes, your body needs food, but it doesn't need to be overfed. The main cause of overeating is not a need for food, but some other problem that means you console yourself with food.

People overeat because they are depressed, lonely, bored, or experiencing other negative feelings. If you are excited, busy, happy, and generally feeling good about yourself, you will be less inclined to snack and overeat.

If your brain is very busy, it hasn't got time to focus or think about food. Follow the plan outlined in this book, start setting goals and feeling happier about yourself, and you will find losing weight will be easier. Don't get me wrong—you should still enjoy your food. I love eating, and going out for a meal with my friends and family is an enjoyable experience. But if you overeat, tackle the negative feelings associated with this bad habit.

The media and advertising have a great deal to do with overeating. Walk down any main street, and you'll see many fast-food outlets and ads for food.

Did you know that fast-food outlets circulate food smells outside the restaurant to get you in? A very clever marketing technique. Supermarkets use the smell of freshly baked bread to make you feel hungry, because it's a fact that hungry shoppers buy more.

If your brain sees an ad for delicious-looking food, it sends a signal that says, "I'm hungry," and then links this to the fast-food outlet that's offering the product.

One of the keys to losing and keeping weight off is to avoid snacks—especially unhealthy ones. If you really need to snack, try nutritious alternatives such as nuts and whole grain crackers.

At this point I should mention diet products, many of which contain artificial sweeteners. I believe these products should be used in moderation, since sweeteners can cause headaches, sugar cravings, and other problems.

I used to be a heavy consumer of diet drinks. In fact, I would buy them by the case. Now I don't buy any diet drinks. I stick to water, fruit juices, and occasionally full calorie drinks.

I have read diet plans that say you can drink unlimited diet drinks, but I believe you're much better off with water.

Overweight Dogs and Owners

I have noticed overweight people also tend to have overweight dogs. They think by overfeeding their dog they are being kind, but they are not. They are killing their pet by passing on their own poor food habits.

My 90 Percent Good, 10 Percent Bad Rule

I don't believe that eating healthily 100 percent of the time is necessary. If you've eaten sensibly for six days and feel like a treat, by all means have one. Looking forward to a treat can motivate you, but make sure your treat isn't so large that it cancels out all your good efforts. Get the order right. Eat sensible foods *first* for most of the week, then have your treat.

An overweight man went to the doctor because he needed to lose weight. The doctor drew up a diet and said that as long as he ate 1,500 calories a day he would lose weight. One month later, the man returned. He weighed more than on the previous visit.

The doctor was baffled. "Did you eat 1,500 calories a day?" he asked.

"Yes," said the man, "but I took advantage of days in the future, too. I'm up to the year 2030!"

A Diet Is for Life

This is the hardest fact to face. If you diet for 1 month, 6 months, or even 12 months and then go back to your old habits, what's going to happen? You'll start putting weight back on again.

The key is to reeducate your eating habits and choose healthy food that is fun and tastes good. With the introduction of healthier convenience meals, pressed nut bars, and vegetable crisps, you can still think you're eating nice foods, even when they are low in calories.

A Few Tips

1. Don't Skip Breakfast

   Eat breakfast like a king, lunch like a prince, and dinner like a pauper.

2. Slow Down

   I used to be a fast eater. I would shovel food down, and, of course, I ended up eating more. Slow down. Using a small desert fork or plate can help.

3. Small Packets

   There's nothing wrong with the odd biscuit, but buy small individual packets or minis. That way, you won't be tempted to finish the whole packet.

4. Get a Blood Test

   If you don't know your blood group, get a blood test and search "blood type diet" on the Internet. The basic premise of this diet is that different blood types should stick to certain foods—in my case, a low amount of meat and dairy.

   On this subject, Dr. Peter D'Adamo has a book called *Eat Right 4 Your Type* (Penguin, 1996), which makes interesting reading.

Summary

A healthy diet does not have to be boring. At the time of writing this book, I have lost over 50 pounds by eating better foods, dealing with my overeating issues, and exercising. As I was 250 pounds before, I've lost around 20 percent of my total body weight.

Losing weight has given me more energy and reduced back pain, meaning I walk better and sit straighter.

Even if you don't need to lose weight, you can still increase your energy levels by watching what foods you eat and taking up regular exercise.

Here's a final word on diet and exercise. It's a sad fact that many people die every year from diseases caused by obesity, smoking, lack of exercise, bad diets, and alcohol.

When you achieve success by following the advice in this book, you will want to live a long and healthy life—so take care of your health. It's important.

Once you get your life into shape and start achieving wealth, you won't want to risk bad health, disease, or death. You'll want to enjoy your new-found success. What could be worse than dropping dead with millions in the bank? I don't think they take credit cards when you cross to the other side!

Here are a few things you may want to add to your Nonmonetary Goals List:

"I want to be fit and active, so I can live for over 100 years."

"I want to invest in diet and exercise now, so I can drive my Ferrari, sail my yacht, and travel the world for as many years as possible."

"I want to take charge of my health and make positive changes."

Dealing with Poor Health

Many illnesses today come from modern living. Our society makes it easy to eat too much, drink alcohol, smoke, and use drugs.

Some illnesses also come from the mind. We are under a lot of stress these days, especially now that mobile phones mean we're always on the go. If you can't turn your mind off, you may well become ill.

Negative thoughts can lead to illness, too, and it is certainly possible to make yourself ill by feeling down about life, worrying, and overreacting to situations.

A sick and negative mind is the worst illness anyone can have—especially if you have real physical problems. Without the power and belief that your body is strong and can recover from anything, you will struggle to overcome illness.

People who feel they have no purpose in life, or are unhappy with their job and surroundings, tend to have more sick days than those who are happy at work and positive about life.

Since owning my own business, which has been going for over 22 years now, I have never had one day off due to illness. Sure, I've had a few coughs and colds, which I have worked through, but that's it.

There is a strong link between mind and body. Keep your mind well, and your body will be well, too.

12

Smart Education and Investing in Yourself

WHEN I WAS AT SCHOOL, I wouldn't be seen dead in a library or bookshop. Now, reading is one of my favorite pastimes. I love learning, and buy many books, training DVDs, and magazines. I also attend seminars and surf the Internet for information.

Information and knowledge are power, and power is priceless. Knowledge is a commodity we all need, and as much as you may already know about a subject, you can always learn more.

Knowledge and education can never be taken away from you. Once it is in your head, it's yours forever. If you were to lose all your possessions in an earthquake tomorrow, you would still have all your knowledge.

Successful People Study

The super-successful are perpetual students. You've heard the saying, THE RICH GET RICHER? It's true. I've sold various how-to information collections, including newsletters and training DVDs, and it never ceases to amaze me that many of the buyers are already very rich and successful.

I have hundreds of doctors, dentists, lawyers, and businesspeople as clients, all of whom are already very successful, yet they still want to know more and are willing to seek and pay for new knowledge.

Use Your Local Library

Most large towns and cities in the UK, Europe, and the United States have excellent libraries, and most are free.

I am very fortunate that my local library is a large one, and offers:

Books (of course)

Magazines (including difficult-to-find trade magazines)

Newspapers (including overseas)

Training DVDs

Audio CDs

Reference directories

Internet access

A great thing about libraries is the librarians. If you ask them nicely, they will try their best to help you however they can. A good librarian is like having a free researcher.

Why a Book Is an Excellent Value

Think about it. Books cost very little, in comparison to training courses or theater tickets, yet they can inform, entertain, and even change your life.

Most people can't afford to hire a successful motivational speaker as their personal tutor for a week. I personally would charge around a hundred times the cost of a book to make this worth my while, yet here in these pages you have hours of my wisdom, and you can refer to it whenever you like for the rest of your life.

I love to read biographies of successful people. It means that, without ever meeting them, I can learn the techniques they used to get to the top.

Buy Books and DVDs, and Attend Seminars

The fact you've invested time and money in this book shows you're already a smart learner and on the way to becoming richer. However, remember this book is only the beginning. Learning is an endless journey.

I strongly advise you to invest in your education. Buying educational books and DVDs, and attending seminars, is never a waste of money.

There are three ways you can obtain business wisdom and life-changing information:

1. The school of hard knocks—i.e., the trial and error method.
2. Find someone who has experienced and overcome the same problem you are facing and quiz her.
3. Buy books, DVDs, and places offering seminars by those who have the kind of success you'd like.

Invest in Other's Success, Not Their Qualifications

There are many theory books available about business. I've read many of them, and they're terrible because the author is a professor who has never done anything except study and lecture.

Let me give you an example. I've read many books about marketing and advertising, a subject which I'm very knowledgeable on. Many of these books contain theories that just don't work in real life. I should know—I've tried them myself.

A good way to tell if you're reading a theory book is to read how the author is introduced.

Which of the following authors would you choose to buy a book from?

A. "Professor Smith is a recognized expert on direct marketing, and has lectured at Oxford University for over 30 years."
B. "Mr. Smith built up a successful direct mail business, starting from only a few hundred dollars in savings, and created a multimillion-dollar business. This book contains many of his top secrets."

You'd choose B, right? Because the author has done it in real life, not just in a classroom.

In books that aren't just theory, the author will tend to refer to their own experiences. For example, "When I was selling," or "I found advertising agencies always. . . ." Professor Smith can't talk that way, because he's never sold anything in his life!

Losers Don't Invest in Education

I have met many businessmen and -women who would be in a far better position if only they'd spent time and money on learning. Instead of investing in themselves, they wasted money on cars, clothes, and gadgets, then they said they don't have any spare money for books or seminars. These people are *losers*!

Knowledge is power. Of course, unless you put that knowledge into practice, it is worthless. But assuming you do, an investment in education will make you a *winner*.

I Know It All and I've Done It All

As you start to gain some success, confidence, and money, you may get complacent. But learning is an endless process. Don't get know-it-all syndrome, just because you've read some good books. You'll have a really *big fall* if you start thinking that way.

Commit to constant learning. Things change, and knowledge becomes out of date. No one ever knows it all—there is always more to learn.

Here is a good example of know-it-all syndrome:

A man sets up a business and it does very well. It feels like he is getting everything right, and the business goes from strength to strength. Inspired by his success, the man sets up another business.

The second business takes him away from the first business, and before he knows it, the first business starts to fail. Times have changed, and he hasn't kept up to date with the first business. He should have invested in books to help him understand how the first business is changing, but he didn't have the time. He spread himself too thinly.

Before long, both businesses fail.

I've seen the above story happen many times in real life. Businesses go up and down. Just because something is going well now doesn't mean it won't require you to learn more at some stage.

I'm not saying you shouldn't be ambitious and confident. Of course you should. That's how you'll get places in life. But understand you are not 100 percent bullet proof, and always make time for further learning—even if you feel your business is going brilliantly and you're master of the universe.

Go the Extra Mile in Everything You Do

One of the key secrets to my success is that I always give a little bit extra in all areas of my life. I've touched on this subject already, but let me now go into more depth.

Many people think, *I want to get by* or *I want to do just enough*. This type of thinking won't make you successful. Get into the habit of giving extra service and going the extra mile, and success will come your way.

Let's take an example. If you work in a supermarket and a customer asks, "Where are the canned tomatoes?" you could say, "Four aisles that way, at the bottom, on the right." That would be perfectly fine. Or you could say, "Let me show you. Follow me." That's going the extra mile. Offering a little bit more doesn't take much effort, and believe me—people appreciate it. Going the extra mile also makes you feel good about yourself. It makes you feel like the good person you truly are.

All businesses involve serving customers in some way or another, and learning how to go the extra mile, whether you're in retail, hospitality, mail order, or Internet selling, will go a long way to making your business a success.

How the Extra Mile Brings Success

Because many people are negatively programmed and go about their life putting in the minimum effort, going the extra mile will make you truly stand out and get ahead. Going the extra mile can be very simple. Work ten extra minutes a day, or hand in some work a little bit earlier than expected. Say "Thank you" to customers, or offer a sincere apology if things have gone wrong. Call people sir or ma'am.

I recently heard about a man who visited a large American store. As he went through the checkout, the cashier handed him his change and receipt, but didn't say thank you. The man was surprised. He said, "You've forgotten to say thank you."

The cashier replied, "It's printed on your receipt."

This story should tell you how little effort many people put into life, and how easy it is to go the extra mile. Saying thank you costs nothing, but can make all the difference.

People and businesses providing that bit extra will always rise to the top. You may not see benefits in the short term, but long term they will always come through.

Whatever your next task is, whether you're a road-sweeper, bank clerk, doctor, or waiter, put a bit extra into your work. Before you know it, you'll benefit both financially and personally.

Whatever profession you are in and however menial you feel your job is, act as though it is the most important job in the world and do it to the best of your abilities.

If a man is called to be a street sweeper, he should sweep streets as

Michelangelo painted, or Beethoven composed music, or Shakespeare

wrote poetry.

He should sweep streets so well that all the hosts of heaven and

earth will pause to say, here lived a great street sweeper who did

his job well.

—Martin Luther King Jr.

One of my very first jobs was keying data into a computer. Most people treated this as a menial and boring job, but I would key data with enthusiasm, accuracy, and skill. I told myself that any one wrong digit would set off World War III, which mentally pushed me to go the extra mile and be as accurate as possible.

Believing Is Seeing

You may think the above title is a typo. After all, isn't the saying, "seeing is believing?" If you don't see it, how can you believe it? But as a matter of fact, I believe there are many times in life when it's better to adopt the "believing is seeing" philosophy.

Faith and *belief* can be stronger than actually seeing something for real. Let me be totally honest with you—this book was finished before the first word was even typed into my computer! It sold 100,000 copies before the first one had even come back from the printers! It was translated into various languages before it had even been finished in English!

So what does this mean? Having faith and belief *first* can help create your reality. Seeing things in your imagination is a great way to make them happen for real.

Without people willing to believe without any hard evidence, many amazing things simply wouldn't exist. There are thousands of people in the pharmaceuticals industry who are working hard to discover cures for AIDS and cancer. These people have faith and belief in their work. There is no evidence they will find a cure, but they still keep going, because they *believe* a cure could exist.

If these people didn't try to find a cure, because they weren't seeing results, this would be disastrous. The world needs believers. Without belief, new cures would never be discovered. Today's trial drugs become tomorrow's reality cures and saviors to millions.

We Reap What We Sow

There is a saying in the Bible: "We reap what we sow." I believe that, regardless of what we do for a living, we're all farmers, and our lives are based on reaping and sowing.

Whether in business, health, love, friendship, or whatever, if you sow hard work, diligence, care, precision, perseverance, faith, and belief into your life, you will reap a bumper harvest. You won't necessarily reap rewards instantly—growing crops takes time—but they will come if you persevere, take care, and water your crop.

If you sow half-heartedly, with fear, doubt, in haste, and carelessly, then you will be lucky to harvest anything, either in the short or long term.

Remember this in everything you do, and you'll become a winning farmer. Your harvest will be everything you truly want out of life.

How to Move a Mountain

In my life I have achieved many truly amazing goals, which, at the outset, felt as impossible as moving mountains. Yet I moved those mountains, single-handedly. Even though, looking back, I feel amazed at what I managed to achieve, I know I could do it again.

Here is my simple formula for moving a mountain. First, work out what resources you have at your disposal. These might be a computer, access to the library, or a friend with the knowledge you need.

Then keep going, a little at a time. It's that simple. Keep going, and take small steps. Whenever you look at your goal and think, "How am I ever going to do that?" just look at the next small step that will take you towards it, and make that step.

When I think of small steps, I always think of ants in cartoons—you know, when they steal a picnic basket? They are tiny, yet hundreds of them together can carry all the food away. People may be tiny compared to a metaphorical mountain, but move it a millimeter at a time and you'll get there. If an ant can move a picnic basket, then believe me, you can achieve anything you set your mind to.

13

Summary to Section One

I HOPE YOU NOW UNDERSTAND the foundations of a successful life, and are beginning to put those foundations in place.

Study Part I as often as you need, and put the principles discussed into action every day. Soon, you will build strong foundations that allow you to build the highest skyscrapers of success, wealth, and happiness.

Scrimp on the foundations, and whatever you build will always be shaky and end up toppling over. Too many people try to make money without understanding the basic principles of putting their life in order first. Without your health, both physical and mental, and a good balanced life style, money will not come your way. Even if it does, it will not fulfill you.

I have disclosed some life-changing tools in this section which, if used correctly, will help you achieve your wildest dreams. However, remember the journey of success requires commitment, perseverance, and vision. There will be obstacles, including the many skeptics you'll meet along the way.

Sometimes, it may feel easier to give up, especially when things don't appear to be going your way, but by giving up and admitting defeat, you join the other millions of life's losers living shallow, empty, and worthless lives and praying for a lottery win.

Success takes effort and courage, but it's absolutely worth it. I speak from first-hand experience.

Remember you have a long way to go yet, and reading the first part of this book is only a tiny step up a long ladder. Yet, you've started climbing. All you need to do is keep going. Make sure you also check my website http://www.themillionairedropout.net as I will post updates and video clips from time to time which will complement what you have learnt from the book.

Now let's find out about making money and fulfilling your financial goals. Combine the new skills you've learned in Part I with the money-making secrets in Part II, and you will become seriously wealthy.

So let's carry on with our incredible journey.

PART

II

Making Money

14

Making Money

In Part I, we explained the importance of setting goals and increasing your self-confidence. Continue with your daily declarations as we enter this next section. It's important you feel positive and confident as we work through Part II, which covers making money.

Self-belief alone is not enough. In this section, I will explain how to put belief into action and start making money.

Part I has prepared your mind. Now Part II will show you how to turn your positive thoughts into action and profit.

Knowledge without action is worthless. You could read this book a thousand times and learn every word by heart, but unless you take action, you won't have success. Unless you *aim* and *fire*, nothing will happen. If you want life to change for the better, you have to *do something*. Talk is cheap, and actions speak louder than words.

Before we go headlong into Part II, remember to look over Part I every so often, and keep in mind the techniques you learned there. This will ensure a positive mental attitude as you progress through Part II.

Just like keeping in physical shape, you should keep exercising your new, healthier ways of thinking. Stop doing physical exercise and you'll soon become unfit. Forget your daily declarations and before you know it, negative thoughts will start creeping in.

Part I represents a lifelong commitment to making your mind and body healthier. Make that commitment, and you're well on your way to creating an amazing life.

Can You Juggle?

Making money is like juggling, but instead of balls and oranges, you need to juggle various areas of your life—mental health, physical health, personal relationships, earning money, and saving money.

Being Your Own Boss

One of the world's richest men, John Paul Getty, said: "You'll never get rich working for someone else." And he's absolutely right. I'm not going to mince my words. The only way you'll make real money is by owning your own business.

I've worked for companies on salaries and commission, and without a doubt running my own business has been much more profitable and enjoyable. Yes, there are some drawbacks to being self-employed, but on balance I guarantee you're better off working for yourself.

As a matter of fact, did you know you're already self-employed? No, you might say. I work for an employer. But you *are* self-employed. You work for *yourself*.

Your employer is just a vehicle for earning money. You work for yourself and your family. Let's be honest—you don't go to work out of the goodness of your heart. If you didn't get paid, I'm sure you wouldn't go in. The truth is, you're working for yourself, but you're giving someone else most of your profits. Start your own business, and you'll get to keep it all.

Why Owning Your Own Business Is the Only Option Today

A few hundred years ago, nearly everyone was self-employed. In fact, if you check back to your grandfather or great-grandfather, chances are they worked for themselves in some capacity. Years ago, most people worked from home in what was known as the cottage industry. Then factories came along, and it all changed. People became employees and relied on companies to look after them.

Right now, many big companies are becoming smaller companies. They're breaking up into smaller divisions, and staff are being laid off. The buzz word for this is *downsizing* or *corporate restructuring*. The truth is, people who have provided a lifetime of loyal service are being laid off.

If you are employed by a large company, you will know your employer demands more and more from you as time goes on. You are asked to come in earlier, work later, and take on increasing responsibility.

In good times, your company rarely increases your pay or benefits, but in bad times it's quick to cut perks or even lay you off. Anyone working in the airline business will know exactly what I mean!

As an employee, you're working just as hard as someone who runs her own business. Yet you're getting none of the freedom or profits that a business owner would.

Take a look at recruitment advertisements, and you'll be amazed what employers expect. For a long list of experience and qualifications, they offer minimal pay and benefits.

I see managing director (MD) jobs advertised offering annual salaries that I can earn in two weeks. The irony is, I wouldn't be offered one of those advertised jobs even if I wanted one (and I don't). Yet here I am, earning much more money and enjoying more freedom than most MDs.

I'm not saying this to gloat—I'm just pointing out how much more rewarding life can be if you own your own business. I'm also trying to show the rewards gap between working for a company and being your own boss—and that's before we've even discussed discrimination in the work place.

Many employers, whatever they tell you, still have old-fashioned ideas about who gets promoted. If you're a woman, have any foreign blood in you (like me), or suffer from a disability, you're better off setting up your own business. Some employers treat everyone equally, but as your own boss you *know* you're being treated equally.

Anyway. Back to history and the cottage industry. These days, things have come full circle. Technology allows us to work from home, so many more people are becoming self-employed again, and this is a good thing.

The rules have changed. The dream is no longer the corner office, a structured career, a gold watch, and a pat on the back at 65. In fact, you probably couldn't even attain that dream, even if you wanted to.

The good news is that technology allows you to run a business from home, the beach, or wherever you desire, while doing what you enjoy and making more money.

I'm sure you've heard the real estate agent saying, "Location, Location, Location"? Well, these days, it doesn't matter half as much. In this virtual age, most businesses can do well anywhere.

Why Starting Your Own Business Is the Key

I left school at 16 with few qualifications and little experience. Working for someone else seemed like my only option, for the time being.

After three years as a salaried employee in the financial sector, I moved to a company in the same sector that paid a salary and commission. I thought this would work well for me, as I would be paid for being a hard worker. Unfortunately, this was in 1987—the year of the big stock market crash. Although I was a good salesman, even I couldn't sell shares to someone after the crash. Many clients had lost thousands of pounds. Some had lost hundreds of thousands. It was then I learned my first important business lesson:

You can't sell something to someone who doesn't have any money.

Sounds simple, doesn't it? But I see companies and shops making this mistake every day. I will explain later how to make sure your potential customer has money.

Anyway, although there was some hope the financial markets would recover, I knew it would take years, and I didn't want to hang around. It was hard to find another job, so I decided I had to make my own job, and started my own business out of necessity.

This was difficult, as I had no business experience and only a few hundred pounds in start-up capital. In other words, my starting position was probably much worse than your current position.

Once you go into business for yourself, there's no going back. You may sell different products or move in different directions over the years, but your days of working for The Man are history.

Are you prepared for a life of calculated risks, sticking your neck out, making mistakes, and being directly responsible for everything that goes wrong? What if I also told you that the rewards will far outweigh the bad times? Running a successful business means wealth, freedom, and health, and in addition to that, just *being* an entrepreneur makes you feel good and proud.

Let me tell you about my sister who, with a little help from me, set up her own business. Her new business involved doing exactly what she *used* to do as an employee. As an employee, she did okay. She earned a good salary and commission, and had a company car. However, we both knew she'd earn far more going it alone.

At her company, my sister earned around £25,000 per year, plus benefits. Not too bad, given this was some time ago. However, in her first year running her own business, she earned over £150,000.

This is a great example of why you should be your own boss. Sure, my sister had to stick her neck out and take risks, but look at what she gained—around six times her original salary.

Now back to you. A few questions . . .

If you're working for a company, are you truly happy with your job?

Are you happy with your income?

Are you being treated as you should?

Is getting to and from work a job in itself?

What would you do if your employer went broke or sacked you tomorrow?

I suggest you take some time to answer each of these questions truthfully. It'll help put your life in a clearer light.

How Did You Choose Your Job?

I've asked hundreds of people this question, and most can't answer. Most people spend very little time choosing their careers and employers. It's usually a case of, "I'll take whatever comes." In fact, many people spend more time choosing a car or house than selecting employment.

Sometimes, people choose a profession because of pressure from parents or other family members (I always wanted to be a teacher, so *you* should become a teacher).

The sad truth is, few people on this earth can truly say they're happy with their job.

My first employee job was at a large bank, where I came across many unhappy workers. They would moan about their pay, conditions, and anything else they could think of, so why did they stay? Because they were too scared or lazy to challenge their employer for a better salary or look for a new job.

I'm sure many of these people are still in the same job and probably still moaning.

Are You in the Wrong Business?

Most people are in the wrong profession, for the reasons already mentioned. To find out if you're in the wrong line of work, answer these questions truthfully:

1. Do you jump out of bed in the morning, eager to go to work, or do you hate going?
2. Do you clock watch and can't wait for the day to end?
3. Are you enthusiastic, motivated, and proud about your work, or only do it because you have to?
4. Do your superiors motivate you and set good examples, or couldn't care less?
5. If you didn't earn any money for what you did, would you still do it?

If you are totally satisfied with your profession, then congratulations. Perhaps your next step is to become a consultant or set up your own business doing the same thing. You could also consider writing a book about your profession, or creating a course. This way, you'll still enjoy what you do, but your income will greatly increase.

If you're not happy with your profession, it's time to get out. It doesn't matter how old you are, or how long you've been in your current job. Don't waste another day. You were clearly never meant to be in that profession in the first place, and you should get out now.

Doing a job you dislike can cause you serious damage. Unhappy people overeat, undereat, smoke excessively, make themselves ill through stress and poor working conditions, and generally cause themselves unnecessary pain and suffering.

What Are Your Skills, and What Makes You Happy?

Let's go back to the drawing board and take stock of *you*.

What skills do you have?

What skills would you like to obtain or improve?

What job or profession would make you jump out of bed in the morning?

Deep down, what was the job or profession you always wanted to do, before others put doubts in your mind?

It's never too late to acquire new skills and move into a profession that truly stimulates and excites you. Obtaining new skills takes time and perseverance, and you may have to attend evening classes after a hard day's work. You may even have to take lower-paid work while you build up new skills, but don't be afraid of making short-term sacrifices for long-term benefits. Improving your life is worth the effort.

Spending your life in the wrong profession really means wasting your life and your talents. You'll never excel in a profession if your heart is not 110 percent in it. Find what you love, and make it your work.

15

Increase Your Income Right Now

RUNNING YOUR OWN BUSINESS IS the key to money, freedom, and happiness, but successful businesses don't happen overnight. If you're employed, I'd suggest remaining so while you set up your business. However, you can still try to increase your current income, right now, in your current job. Let me tell you how.

Asking for a Pay Raise

The quality and quantity of the service you render, plus the attitude with which you render it, determine the amount of pay you get and the sort of job you hold.

—Dr. Napoleon Hill

Be honest with yourself. How much money do you deserve in your current job? Look at your own work, your attendance, and your contributions. Are you putting 65 minutes into an hour, or just coasting by? How much money are you making for your organization?

Imagine you're the CEO of your company. Would you be happy and delighted with your performance and service?

If you're not giving your job 110 percent, then I'm afraid you don't deserve a pay raise. If you do no more than what you're paid to do, you have no basis for requesting more money. You're already getting all

116

you deserve. You need to deliver extra benefits before you can ask for extra pay.

Some people might say a pay raise would make them work harder, but it doesn't work like that. You have to put in the work first, before you receive the rewards.

If you strongly believe you have an excellent case for a pay raise, then go ahead and challenge your employer for a higher salary.

If you are coasting by, be happy with what you're getting and put your efforts into your new business.

Preparing a Case for a Pay Raise

Write a letter about why you feel you're entitled to a pay raise or better job position. Stick to the facts, and use positive, upbeat language. Then ask for a meeting with the relevant person in your organization, and before the meeting—preferably the night before—use the declaration technique and say, "I have increased my wage by . . ." and use a specific amount. Visualize yourself in the meeting. You are smiling, calm, and in control. Visualize yourself being given the pay raise.

On the day of the meeting, stay calm, speak slowly and clearly, sit up straight, and demand what you deserve. Hand over a copy of the letter you have prepared, and go over its contents, explaining in positive, confident language why you deserve a pay raise.

Important!

Don't tell anyone in your organization (even your closest work friends) what you're doing. Whether you get a pay raise or not is between you and your employer. Many employers worry that if they give you a pay raise, they'll have to give everyone else one, too. Keeping quiet, both before and after your meeting, will eliminate that problem.

The Outcome

A Positive Answer

If the answer is yes, then well done! You've increased your salary. Continue working hard, but remember that having your own business is your ultimate goal. It's good to increase your salary, but working for someone else still isn't acceptable.

A Neutral Answer

Your employer may agree that you're worth more, but is not able to pay you extra at this time. This is where you need to start bargaining. Suggest things you'll accept instead of money, such as a better job title, training course, extra paid holidays, better company car, and so on. Even if you gain an extra $10 a week in lunch expenses, you've walked away with something.

A No Answer

It's a shame your employer doesn't value your talents. You haven't lost anything by asking and you're not the loser—your employer is. It's important to stay calm. Tell your employer, either in person or by letter, that you're very disappointed, but you will continue to work at your best level and hope a review can be made in the future.

In many ways, you're in the same position as you would have been with a positive answer. Your ultimate goal is still to aim for your own business.

Summary

If you don't ask, you don't get. Most companies won't spontaneously offer you an extra $100 a month for no apparent reason. You need to make the first move. Yes, it takes courage, but with good preparation and using the techniques outlined in this book, you can do it. Whichever way it goes, you're a winner for asking. If you get a pay raise—you win. If you don't, you know where you stand, and the fact you tried makes you a winner anyway.

If things don't go your way, don't make threats you're not willing to carry out. If you *are* prepared to quit your job, don't say, "I'm walking out today." Soften the threat by saying, "This leaves me in a very difficult position, and I will have to consider my options."

Sometimes, emotions overcome common sense, but please *think* before you say something you may regret. Pause for thought. The same goes with e-mails. Once you've hit the Send button, there's no going back. If you're sending a difficult e-mail, write a draft, save it, and come back for another think before you press Send.

If you do end up quitting, leave your employer on good terms. It's a small world, and there may come a time when you need to do business with them, or ask a favor.

Are You Too Comfortable?

It's probably wise to keep your current employment while you're getting started in business, but don't make the mistake of feeling too comfortable. Just because you've still got your day job to fall back on doesn't mean failure is acceptable. You *must* succeed.

Some people claim to work better under pressure, and in truth, when I started my business I was under serious pressure. I had to make it work almost immediately, and I did. If I'd had the comfort of another income, I might not have achieved this success.

If you don't have a current employer, you may discover this is a real blessing. Not having any money coming in scared me into success. I'll talk more later about why having too much start-up capital can be a disadvantage. Yes—I did say disadvantage.

16

Starting Your Own Business

I F YOU HAVE A DAY job, you'll need a business that is flexible and can be run after hours, from home, on a small budget. However, this doesn't mean thinking small. You want a business that can grow and expand with your needs and aspirations.

Most businesses are doomed to fail because they need staff, premises, a large initial outlay, face-to-face customer contact, and professional licenses or qualifications.

However, I'll teach you how to start a business with none of these things.

Staff? You can do everything yourself, or outsource to freelance contractors.

Premises? Thanks to the Internet and the fact you can rent call answering services at low cost, you can be open 24 hours a day. You can genuinely make money while you're sleeping.

Huge outlay? My model requires no franchise, stock, or furniture. Your outlay will be tiny and highly affordable.

Face-to-face customer contact? My business model means never dealing with anyone face to face. You may like meeting customers, but it's far more productive not to.

Professional qualifications and red tape? My model allows you to work from home, without red tape, or health and safety requirements.

The traditional business/retail model that requires premises and huge outlay is becoming extinct. I'm going to teach you about mail-order/Internet commerce, which is a business model that is going from strength to strength. Here's why.

1. People are more comfortable than ever before about buying online or over the phone with a credit or debit card.
2. Technology is getting easier and cheaper. Building a website can now be done in a few hours, without technical skills, and many technological tools can now be obtained cheaply or for free. Sites like http://www.1and1.com make it simple for anyone to get a professional website running in a few hours.
3. These days, even the smallest business can sell to a global market. I have customers in 109 countries, and thanks to reliable couriers I can ship and sell all over the world. Better still, electronic downloads require no shipping.
4. Anyone can now publish a book or sell a product on Amazon. The barriers to entry have gone. You don't need a book publisher to sell to a huge audience. Anyone can advertise on search engines like Google, and anyone can sell on eBay. Just think how incredible that is. You can stand on the shoulders of these giant companies. This is a glorious time to be an entrepreneur.

If I have seen farther, it is by standing on the shoulders of giants.
—Isaac Newton

The Best Business Model in the World

What is the best business model in the world? It's a model I owe everything to. I came into it without understanding what I was doing, and started from my bedroom with a few hundred pounds. I built up various businesses, using this model, that were soon worth hundreds of thousands of pounds.

This business model has been around for many years (way before the Internet was popular), and will continue to thrive. It is truly the last business where the little man or woman can compete with large multinationals and beat them.

What is this business model?

Mail order.

You can also call it direct marketing or Internet marketing. There is probably no other business model in the world where so many men and women (including me) have started from scratch and become millionaires, and even billionaires.

I could list thousands of names and companies that owe everything to mail order. The list would include Sir Richard Branson of The Virgin Group, who started selling records via mail order, advertising in student magazines, and working from a tiny apartment. It would also include the late Anita Roddick, who founded the Body Shop. She started by selling a few beauty products and advertising them in teenage magazines. My list could go on and on. . . .

What's So Great about Mail Order?

The lifestyle and riches that a mail-order business can bring are beyond your wildest dreams. With mail order, you can choose the hours you work—perhaps three months of the year, with the rest of the year off. You can work from the comfort of your own home and operate in your pajamas. You can live anywhere in the world, even the middle of nowhere.

Mail order offers choice, freedom, and no ceiling on earnings. You can start an enterprise from your kitchen, and it can grow (like Virgin and the Body Shop) into a worldwide business.

What Mail Order Is Not

Mail order is not a get-rich-quick scheme. However, if you get the right product, you can make it big very quickly. It's also not an opportunity to deceive people and sell shoddy goods. Please don't confuse mail order with multilevel marketing or chain letters or any other home business scam you may have read about.

Mail order is a legitimate and well-established business model that I am proud to be associated with. The key to my success and yours is building up good client relationships and a client list you can revisit to offer new products and services. If you rip people off or provide bad value, it's not possible to sell to them again.

Before you think mail order sounds hopelessly out of date in the Internet age, let me correct you. The Internet has added power to mail order, but the fundamentals of the business model are the same. Lucky for you, the Internet has made things even easier, and gives you advantages I never had when I started 25 years ago.

This Business Model Is Global

The great news about the mail-order business model is that you can operate from anywhere and sell to anywhere. It doesn't matter where you live. I have operated this business from all over the world, even on a ship. I've been spending dollars and earning pounds, and vice versa. And I've sold goods all over the world. It truly doesn't matter where you are—there are few geographical barriers with mail order.

KISS—Keep It Simple, Stupid

I'm sure you've heard this before, but after over 27 years in business, I can tell you that, on the whole, it's simple. I'm not saying it's all going to be easy, but it probably won't be as hard as you think. I'm not that smart (truthfully!), and I believe this has worked in my favor because I've kept things simple.

I was recently talking to Simon Woodroffe (the founder of Yo! Sushi, Yotel, and an original dragon from Dragons' Den) about what would have happened if we'd been very academic and scrutinized all the ins and out of starting our businesses. Our conclusion? We would never have started!

What You Need to Succeed in Mail Order

The key skills, talents, and resources you'll need for success are:

- Self-discipline and determination.
- A desire to succeed.
- A desire to develop the hidden talents you never get to use.
- The ability to adapt and think quickly.
- The ability to learn new techniques and copy successful formulas.

- The ability to multitask. (One minute you'll be on your computer, the next you'll be answering the phone, packing goods, or sending out mail shots. An hour later you might then be researching products and designing ads.)
- Flexibility.
- A willingness to do whatever it takes to succeed. You'll be the only employee for a while, so if the bin needs emptying, or a heavy sack of mail needs carrying to the post office, you can't say it's not your job. *Everything* is your job in the early days.

I can't promise you money for nothing. I *can* promise you a legitimate business that will earn as much money as you want. I *can* promise you a business that will give you freedom and a great lifestyle. You *can* truly stick it to The Man, and never have to deal with office politics and hierarchy that sucks the life out of you.

Money may come very quickly for you. However, I hope it doesn't come too quickly. When you earn money over time, it will *taste* a lot better than if you inherit it or win the lottery.

Back in 1999, I had a few of my acquaintances strike it rich in the dot.com boom. They became multimillionaires overnight (well, at least on paper). However, within two years most had lost their new-found wealth. Easy come, easy go.

To succeed in this, or any other business, you need to really *want* success, and this is proved over time, not overnight.

People who succeed in business plan for success. They have goals and move towards them. Not everybody who plans for success achieves it right away, but those who really *want* success, and are prepared to adapt and change as they learn more about the marketplace, will succeed. The retail dinosaurs that have recently gone bust did not adapt.

Being adaptable is important. Because mail-order businesses are, at their heart, small, they can adapt very quickly. Like a small speed boat, small businesses can make sharp turns, whereas big corporate warships take miles to turn around.

Just Do It

Soon, I will disclose a great deal of information about how to get your business up and running. I will share with you as many secrets as I can.

However, there is something you must do. *Put my advice into practice* as quickly as possible. Not all at once, of course. I don't expect you to be perfect. What I expect is that you *start*.

Perhaps you're thinking, *I can't start yet, I don't know everything*. Good research and planning are important, but so is just going for it.

In Part I, you'll recall I listed the many excuses people give for *not* taking action. Those same excuses are used every day by people who never start their own business or who drop out when the going gets tough. Please don't be one of them.

Contrary to popular belief, starting something badly, or in a small way, is better than doing nothing. If you keep putting off starting your business until you know everything about everything, you will never start.

Here is a classic quote that sums up my argument:

Better to do something imperfectly than to do nothing flawlessly.
—R.H. Schuller

Very true. When I started my business, I had far less knowledge than you will have after reading this book. My circumstances forced me to start, even though I wasn't ready, but I don't regret it. Looking back, I cringe at some of the mistakes I made in the early days, but at least I started. I was a player, not a spectator, and that's the difference between me and most other people.

I was always crazy enough to believe in what I was doing and crazy enough to dream. I kept going, even through low points and setbacks, as I knew I was doing the right thing and believed I would be rewarded one day.

I'm Not a Textbook Businessman

I'm proud to say I'm a *real* businessman. I'm not stiff, pompous, or theory based. All the advice I'll give you has been tried out in the real world. If you want the theory on how business works, go to the library or a business bookshop, and you will find hundreds of guides to starting your own business.

On the whole, these books are terrible, and the easiest way to fail at business is to follow their advice. They are normally written by people who have never made any money in business. They're spectators who have never played the game.

The information I will share in these pages is not about what *should* happen in business. It's about what *does* happen in business. If you were going to war, would you follow someone who'd researched a war, or someone who'd just fought and won a war? Come to war with me and I'll show you the real secret weapons you need.

Now back to business. . . .

What *Is* Mail Order?

Mail order means supplying goods and/or services to clients who've never seen you or your product. The initial contact comes through an ad, sales letter, article, blog post, or Internet search that invites the customer to find out more and/or buy your product.

The customer either phones the order through or places an order online. You process the order and send the goods, either by mail or, in most cases today, by courier. These days, the Internet makes up a large part of marketing products, and, increasingly, your customers will order online rather than by phone.

If you're selling via someone like Amazon, they can deal with all order taking and shipping. Digital books can all be dealt with by a company such as clickbank.com, where the whole process is automated.

You can purchase almost anything by mail or online, including books, DVDs, computers, clothes, toys, furniture, vitamins, loans, adult-oriented goods, fitness equipment, food, and flowers.

Mail-order shopping has exploded in popularity because it is so convenient and easy for the shopper. There has also been a change in the customer's attitude to direct mail and online shopping. Today's shoppers are happy to buy goods from strangers based hundreds of miles away, and nearly everyone has a phone, Internet access, and a credit or debit card.

Two hundred years ago, nobody could or would buy anything via mail order. Shoppers visited a local store and bought products from someone they knew. In many cases, they would barter. No one had a phone or credit card, and there wasn't a reliable postal service. Think how lucky you are to be living in this golden age, where shopping and selling are so easy.

Offering Consultancy and Agency Services by Mail Order

Some mail-order businesses offer goods. Others offer consultancy and agency services. The basics and principles are the same for both, but consultants and agencies offer a service, rather than a product, so are essentially middlemen.

Let's take the example of a recruitment agency. The agency is a middleman between the prospective employee and the employer. The agency earns a fee for introducing a candidate to an employer. There is no product being sold, but the basic principles are the same as for a product-based mail-order business.

Consultancy means offering expert advice to companies on your chosen subject. This could be marketing, motivation, advertising, and so on. The product, in this case, is *you*. I know people who've quit their jobs to become consultants in the same business—and sometimes even been rehired by their ex-employers. The story is always the same. They ended up earning much more money going it alone.

Getting Started in Mail Order

To be taken seriously in business, you need your own domain name and e-mail address. Don't use Gmail, Yahoo!, Hotmail, or any other free e-mail service—it screams amateur.

Setting up a domain name and e-mail is cheap and easy. You can use a company such as godaddy.com or easily.co.uk, and their website will walk you through the process. The domain name you choose will become your e-mail address. So http://www.thespreadtrader.com becomes vince@thespreadtrader.com and sales@thespreadtrader.com. I'm sure you'll agree these e-mail addresses look far better than vince@hotmail.com.

Your domain name should reflect your business, be short, and avoid hyphens and difficult-to-spell words. In time, you are likely to have many domain names, but start with one or two. Visit http://www .domainit.com for a great suggestion tool that finds domain names based around certain keywords.

You should also set up a YouTube channel, Twitter account, and Facebook page to reflect your business. These can all be created for free. Even if you have your own personal Twitter or Facebook account, set up new ones for business and keep them separate. If I'm interested in buying your product, I really don't want to read about what you did on the weekend.

You should also set up a blog platform. My favorite is http://www .wordpress.com. WordPress has many features and third-party plug-ins that allow you to build a very professional site/blog. A more professional (self-hosted) version with your own domain name costs a few dollars a month, and is worth the investment. Have a look at http://www.mysite .com, which offers a very simple WordPress hosted facility.

Company Structure

For tax purposes, you need to choose a legal framework for your business. I'd recommend starting as a Sole Proprietor or Trader. When your business grows, you can look at other options. In the United States, a Sole Proprietor reports his or her income on Schedule C of the 1040 tax form.

Setting Up a Bank Account

You need a business bank account to receive earnings and pay company expenses. A business bank account is totally separate from your personal account, even if you're trading under your own name.

Opening a business account is fairly simple. Most banks are desperate for your business and will offer *free* banking for at least a year. You can either open a business account with your existing bank (depending on your current standing with them) or start afresh with a new one. I will talk more about banks, accepting credit cards, and borrowing money later.

Always remember: your bank works for you. They are your servant, not vice versa. Of course, you should talk to bank employees in a friendly and courteous way (whether they're junior cashiers or senior managers), but expect and demand the highest level of service and respect in return.

You should be addressed as sir or ma'am, and nothing should be a problem. Just because you're small fry today doesn't mean you won't be a big fish tomorrow. Over time, a bank can make a lot of money from you, and they should treat you well from day one.

On the subject of banks, many people think they're in business to provide a service to the community, or they're some sort of government body. This is not the case. Banks exist for one reason, and that's to make money. They have no morals, feelings, or loyalty to anyone other than directors and shareholders.

Letter-Headed Paper/Online Signature

You must be seen as a serious business, and this means a professional letterhead. A letterhead may not seem too important to you, but it's the first contact most of your clients, contacts, and customers will have with your company.

If your letterhead doesn't build confidence in your ability to get the job done, it will cost you business. It's very important you not look like a one-man band. Just because you're working from a studio apartment doesn't mean you can't appear as big as IBM.

Your letterhead can also be used as your electronic e-mail signature. This means creating a version of it that can be attached to an e-mail template.

Creating a Letterhead

Here are some great websites that make creating a letterhead easy.

In the United States: http://www.fedex.com/us/office/

In the UK: http://www.vistaprint.co.uk

These sites offer lots of other services for small businesses, too.

Letterhead Rules

1. Letterheads should have a clean, uncluttered look.
2. The font (typeface) should be easy to read, and the company name, address, telephone number, fax number, and e-mail address/web address must be written clearly.
3. Don't make your letterhead look like a rainbow. Too many colors do not look good and end up costing more money to print. Use two colors, such as blue and red, or black and green. You can also use tints if you wish.

4. Formulate company colors and a logo or typeface style that you can carry throughout your business. Look at what other big companies are using. A one-man/woman business can still have a corporate image.
5. Use white paper (it makes black text stand out better). In layman's terms, paper should be thicker than photocopier paper, but not so thick you need a crow bar to fold it. Very thick paper is a total waste of money. It's what solicitors use, and I imagine is probably part of the reason they charge such huge fees.
6. Don't choose a raised paper. Laser printers don't like it, and the heat from the printer can make it crack.
7. If you're a Limited Company, you'll need to put the company registration number and registered address etc. at the bottom of the paper.

A good letterhead won't be as expensive as you think. Print a small quantity to start with (normally 500), and take it from there.

Shop around for printing prices, as there can be big variations. A cheap quote is vital, but don't sacrifice quality for the sake of a few dollars. Some back-street printers use old machinery that produces awful results.

Business Cards

A business card is an essential item to carry in your wallet or purse. It should have your details on it, just like a letterhead, and your name in a clear font with your title underneath.

It's also a good idea to print a brief description of what your company does on the back of the card.

Virtual Phone Numbers

You can now get a phone number that can be redirected to any other number for a reasonable charge. This gives you a landline number, without the extra expense. A cell-phone number doesn't look professional, and many customers will be put off calling it.

In the United States, try http://www.flynumber.com

In the UK, try http://www.dmclub.net (they've been established for over 17 years)

Fax

Fax is not as big as it was some years ago, and it's on its way out. I don't think you need to bother with a fax machine, but you can still get a fax number. I use Efax, which allows me to send and receive faxes directly from my computer. Check Efax.com.

Mailing Address

This is a big stumbling block for most home businesses. A residential address doesn't look good on a company letterhead. The simple solution is to use a business center, sometimes known as a serviced office. I don't advise using a P.O. box, as it makes you look fly-by-night.

Business Centers

A business center gives you a permanent office address, without the physical space of an office. All your posts and messages are held for you, and can either be posted to your home address, or picked up in person.

Business centers offer an excellent service and are ideal for the home business user. Most business centers offer many other services, such as word processing, outgoing post handling, faxing, and photo-copying. You can also hire an office or boardroom by the day (or in some cases, by the hour), which is perfect for any meetings you don't want to hold at home.

Regus has a network of business centers all over the world, which can be useful if you're based in the United States, but want a UK address/office or vice versa. Here is their website: http://www.regus.com/.

In the UK, you might also like to try: http://www.mwbex.com/.

Wherever you are in the world, there's likely to be a business center in the nearest big city.

NOTE: If you choose to divert your calls to a business center when you're out, it's better to have a live person answer your phone—especially during office hours. If you use voicemail, make sure your voice is professional. For a professional voiceover, try http://www.fiverr.com.

Accepting Credit and Debit Cards

Today, people pay for most things by credit or debit card. I strongly recommend you set up merchant facilities to accept Visa, MasterCard, American Express, Discover (U.S.) and debit cards.

You must make it as easy as possible for a customer to buy, and credit/debit cards are much quicker and more convenient than check or bank transfer.

Of course, there are a few disadvantages to accepting credit cards. First, there's a fee per transaction, which is around 4 percent on credit cards and $2 per transaction on debit cards for start-ups. Second, you're liable for charge backs, which means if there's a problem with the credit card, you may have to refund the credit card company.

I've accepted credit cards for many years, and although you may experience a few fraudulent transactions, the benefits far outweigh the disadvantages. In mail order, you have to be more vigilant than most, as you won't physically see the credit card you're taking payment from. However, you can take steps to reduce credit card losses, and credit card issuers will give you some good guidance notes.

Companies offering merchant facilities to small businesses include:

http://www.worldpay.com

http://www.paypal.com

http://www.barclaycard.co.uk/business/

Your bank can also advise on where to find small business merchant facilities.

At this point, I'd like to make something clear. It's a *privilege* to accept credit cards, not a *right*. Banks don't have to provide this facility. Remember this throughout your negotiations, and you'll get on fine.

Credit card companies may be wary of you, especially in the early days, as many banks have suffered huge losses through fraudulent credit card transactions. People can quite easily set up a merchant account, charge up thousands of pounds in orders, forget to deliver the goods, and skip town. The credit card company must then refund all their cardholders.

I hope everyone reading this is honest and in business for the long-term benefits. However, there are unscrupulous people out there, and thanks to these idiots (most of whom get caught) the rest of us have to suffer.

If you sell on Amazon, Clickbank, or eBay, you won't need your own merchant facilities. This is also true if you're an affiliate for another company. In this instance, the company will process the credit cards and pay you a commission. However, it's likely you'll want to make your own direct sales at some stage, and to process cards via telephone, mail order, and Internet sales. These days you won't need a credit card terminal, as everything can be done online. You will be given special secure software that allows you to process payments using your computer.

Borrowing Money

I'm not a fan of borrowing money. I believe if you have to borrow money to start a business, it's a bad business. Fortunately, the business model I'm showing you requires very little start-up capital.

Every one of my businesses has been started with my own money—either from savings, or money earned from another business. The only time I've ever borrowed money was for a mortgage on an apartment, which I used as my office and home. A sensible investment, I'm sure you'll agree.

Today, I'm fortunate enough not to have a mortgage. That is something you should all aim for. Owning your house outright gives a great sense of security. If everything goes wrong, you still have somewhere to sleep at night.

Back to borrowing money. I suggest you use your own savings and avoid raising any money from friends and family. If you don't have savings, start making some.

Stand-By Credit Cards and Overdrafts

As I mentioned in Part I, I used to be a worrier, and still am to a degree. My anxious side means I still have access to large amounts of credit, should I ever need it.

I suggest you also have some credit to fall back on, just in case things don't go as planned or your timing is slightly out. In the saving money section, I will tell you who the best credit card companies are.

Using credit cards can be useful, but they can also make a situation worse. Think carefully before using credit. Will it give you enough breathing space to make things better, or will it makes things temporarily better, but worse in the long term? Let's look at a few scenarios.

Scenario 1

Your business is not going well.

If things are going badly and your business is failing, it would be foolish to run up credit debts. Throwing money at a problem does not cure it. *Why* is your business failing? Chances are the reason is about much more than money.

Scenario 2

Business is genuinely going well. However, due to a few factors that you didn't calculate, you have a temporary shortfall.

Don't kid yourself here. Will the shortfall *really* be temporary? Look back over your past few months of business. Is there proof that things will get better?

Scenario 3

A genuine opportunity has come up to buy stock or equipment at a reduced price—for example, at an auction, where payment is required immediately.

In this scenario, I would suggest you use temporary credit, as long as the saving equals more than the interest you'll pay.

Once you're in credit debt, your number one goal is to pay off that debt as quickly as possible. Interest rates can cost a fortune, but if you settle the balance quickly, you will pay little or nothing.

When you buy something on a credit card, you get up to 50 days' interest-free credit, which may just be long enough to pay back the borrowed amount. This does not work on cash advances, as most credit cards charge interest from day one.

There are advantages to credit cards. It's very quick and simple to settle a credit card debt, and you can pay back in variable amounts. For example, if you take an advance of $2,000, pay back the minimum amount in the first month, then the balance in the second, you won't receive any penalty or interest.

In comparison, a loan with a lower interest rate has a fixed payment schedule. Although you can pay the loan off early, most banks charge early redemption penalties that can be very high.

An overlooked way to finance a purchase is trade credit. Most business suppliers issue 30-day invoices, giving you 30 days to pay.

Most people think they need capital so they can start big. I can tell you from experience that you're better off starting small and building up.

Here's a staggering fact. Richard Branson of the Virgin Group owns around 120 different companies, including Virgin Atlantic Airways, Virgin Holidays, and Virgin Media. Almost all these companies were started from scratch, meaning Branson didn't buy an existing business— he created a successful money-making venture from the bottom up. In many cases, he used very little start-up capital. His airline business began on a small budget, and he leased old planes at first, upgrading to newer ones as profits came in.

So the next time you think, *If only I had more start-up capital*, think again. You must stay *lean* and *hungry*.

17

Finding Products to Sell

LET'S START WITH WHAT YOU don't want to sell. You don't want to go into competition with Tesco or Wal-Mart. We're not interested in low margins or price wars. You want high margin products that are relatively easy to ship. You also want simple products that don't require lots of technical support. These include books (print and electronic), DVDs, audio CDs, jewelry, gift items, and niche markets.

There are three ways to find products:

1. *Produce your own product.* This is the most advantageous product-sourcing method, as it means you keep all the profits. You can also outsource some of the production. For example, if you're writing a course on how to start a window cleaning business, you can pay someone else to do the writing.
2. *Buy low-cost products in bulk, then resell them.* You could, for example, buy fashionable handbags from the Far East (but *not* designer fakes), and resell them in the United States or UK.
3. *Act as an affiliate or drop ship.* This can be okay to begin with, but as an affiliate you only get a small percentage of the sale. Often, you won't get paid any ongoing commission.
4. *Buy reprint and resale rights.* You can buy the rights to reprint and sell books and reports, without paying the author any further commission. If you take a look at http://www.master-resale-rights .com or search "PRL resell," you will find plenty of sources.

In reality, you may do all four of the above, and mix and match. For example, you might part-write an eBook and merge it with one you have bought the reprint rights to. Or buy the reprint rights to an eBook, change the title and have a new cover designed. Yes—people do judge a book by its cover. You can find some great, inexpensive cover designers on http://www.fiverr.com.

Don't become overwhelmed. Take small, manageable steps every day. You can eat an elephant if you take it a bite at a time.

Research

The biggest mistake most people make in business is doing little or no research into the product they're selling and the market they're selling to.

Look at any main street, and you'll see new businesses come and go very quickly. The story normally goes like this.

Joe Public loses his job and has a few thousand dollars. He opens a shop, gets advice on sorting out tax and business bank accounts, but forgets the most important thing—*making money from customers*.

You see, Joe Public hasn't done any research. He doesn't know what the market wants. He sells at the wrong price, goes broke, and puts it down to bad luck. My advice is, forget about tax and accountants in the beginning, because if you don't sell anything, you won't have any tax to pay!

Focus on finding and reaching your target market. Sell the right product at the right profit margin, then hire the best accountants and solicitors with your profits.

The Market Will Make or Break You

Unless we identify our market *before* we go into business, we'll end up like Joe Public. We need to put the market first and product second. We need to know how people think, and what they want and feel.

What people buy today is not the same as 10 or even 2 years ago. Buying habits depend on current news, politics, and many other things—even the movies. When *Jurassic Park* came out, it trebled sales of wooden dinosaur kits at the Natural History Museum. Suddenly, everyone became interested in dinosaurs.

You may not be in the dinosaur business, but if you know what is going on around you, you can source products that will sell. Using the Internet can give you a vast amount of free facts and figures about what people want to buy right now.

The late Gary Halbert (a top marketing guru) addressed a seminar in the United States many years ago. He asked the audience to imagine they had a hamburger stand, and he had a stand in competition with them. He would allow them any advantages they cared to name, and he only wanted one advantage.

The audience asked for advantages such as the best meat, the best position, and the biggest stand. Gary said they could have all those things. All he wanted was one advantage, which no one had mentioned, and he would beat them easily.

"What can it be?" the crowd asked.

"Easy," said Gary. "The only advantage I need is a *hungry crowd!*"

Remember that word—*hungry*. Vast fortunes have been lost, and many companies have gone broke, because they tried to sell products that weren't wanted. No one was hungry for them.

On the subject of Gary Halbert, his site is still live and well worth checking out for some very good marketing tips. See http://www.thegaryhalbertletter.com.

Of course, with enough time and money, you can use the media, press, and television to convince people they need something.

Take the example of deodorant. It took nearly 20 years and literally millions of dollars of advertising revenue to convince people they must have it. Now, it sells everywhere, but you and I don't have the time or budget to convince people they want something brand new.

Picking Easy Targets

Unlike most people, I'm not in the business of reinventing the wheel. I don't care if I'm not the first to think of a business. In most cases, I would prefer to be second or third. What I do want, and what you should be looking for, are easy targets—markets that are desperate for what we are selling. Your buyers must be *hungry*.

The biggest mistake most companies make is spending too much time and money developing a product, then say, "Who shall I sell this to?"

Instead of going to your market and saying, "This is what I have for sale—do you want to buy it?" you should be able to say, "Here's your chance to get the product you've desperately been looking for."

Having exactly what the market wants is a sure way to achieve success in business. If you want to buy a car and I try to sell you a boat, we're going to have a difficult time. If I have a book on trading and investing, and you're interested in needlework, you're clearly not my customer. You need to make sure people want your product, and then *sell* to those people.

People Buy What They Want, Not What They Need

Read that title again—it's important. People buy what they *want*, not what they need. Let's be honest—nobody needs a Ferrari, Bentley, or Maserati. People buy these cars because they *want* one.

Let me give you another example. Most people *need* life insurance and health care insurance, but they don't have it. Why not? Because they don't want it. People don't want to think about death or illnesses, and that's why life insurance is hard to sell.

In the next few pages, I'll give you specific products and markets you can sell them to. I have successfully sold these products myself, and you can too.

Where to Start Your Research

Google is a great place to start, and it's free. The search engine collects a massive amount of data. You can look at Google Trends, which shows what people are searching for, but a better way to understand market desires is to set up a free Google AdWords account.

Adwords is the advertising program run by Google. I'm sure you've noticed the small text ads that come up when you search a topic (to the right and at the top of the page). See Figure 17.1.

They're called pay-per-click ads, and an AdWords account will help you set these up. However, you don't need to set up an ad to discover what people are searching for. AdWords gives you a free keyword tool that helps you find this out.

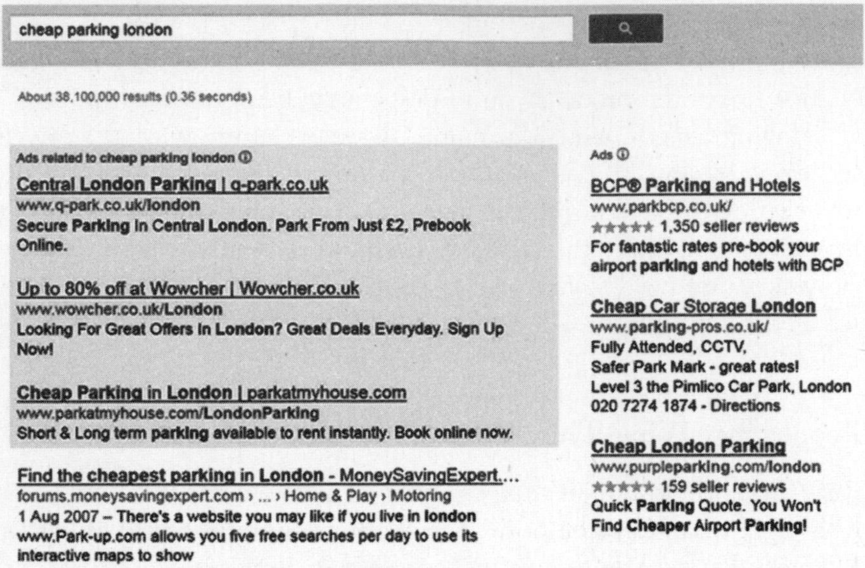

Figure 17.1

Type in a few experimental words, and the keyword tool will tell you all the things people typed into Google, based around those words. You'll find people searching for "will my ex come back," "organic dog food," and even, "how to teach my parrot to talk."

Discovering what people are searching for helps us identify what the market wants. Google will also tell you *how many* people are searching for any given term, so you can work out if the market is big enough to bother with.

Now let's think about how to offer products to these hungry buyers. For example, a sample search for "golf swing" shows 450,000 searches for this term in one month. So what can we sell these buyers? A course, DVD, or newsletter on how to get the perfect swing. See Figure 17.2.

eBay—What People Are Buying

eBay is no longer just an auction site, selling bric-a-brac. Today, it's more of a department store, and most products on sale are brand new. We'll discuss later how you can sell on eBay, but for now let's continue talking about research.

Keyword		Competition	Global Monthly Searches [?]	Local Monthly Searches [?]
☐	golf swing ▾	Low	450,000	450,000
⊞	✓Save all **Perfect (14)** · perfect golf swing, the perfect golf swing...			More like these
⊟	✓Save all **Golf Video (58)**		More like these	1 - 10 of 68 [?] ‹ ›
Keyword		Competition	Global Monthly Searches [?]	Local Monthly Searches [?]
☐	golf swing video ▾	Low	14,800	14,800
☐	perfect golf swing video ▾	Low	590	590
☐	golf swing videos ▾	Low	5,400	5,400
☐	golf swing video slow motion ▾	Low	590	590
☐	slow motion golf swing video ▾	Low	590	590
☐	free golf swing videos ▾	Medium	170	170
☐	golf swing video recorder ▾	Medium	110	110
☐	golf video swing ▾	Low	14,800	14,800
☐	natural golf swing video ▾	Medium	58	58
☐	the perfect golf swing video ▾	Low	590	590

Figure 17.2

You can use eBay to find out what people are buying. Visit http://www.hotlister.com for a great tool that tells you what people are bidding on. You can refine your search to country and sector. For example, books in the United States, or baby products in Canada.

If I go to hotlister and see thousands of users watching an item, I know this is a product people want. It's fascinating to see what's selling and how things are changing. For example, a short while ago, hair extensions were a top seller. I'd never have known that without research.

By looking at what others are buying, you identify a hungry crowd.

Bestseller Book Lists

Looking at bestselling book lists gives you an idea of the topics people want to read about. Of course, these days many books are sold as eBooks. You can see the eBook bestsellers on Amazon's Kindle Store. We're interested in *nonfiction*, as these books give us a great idea of popular interest and therefore buying trends.

Shopping Channels

The top shopping channels like QVC, HSN, and Ideal World know what they're doing. If you're watching QVC and see eight hours of programming dedicated to jewelry, you know jewelry is selling well. As it happens, QVC does devote a lot of time to selling jewelry, and it *is* a big seller with high profit margins.

Be Alert and Watch Trends

Remember I said you make your own luck in life? Increase your luck by being alert to new opportunities, changing trends, and what people are buying or concerned about. Then think about how you can profit from this, and you'll be amazed by how lucky you become.

Instead of searching Google as a consumer, start using the Internet for its marketing tools. The next time you type something into the Google search bar, stop midsentence and see what Google thinks you're going to ask. Google has a prediction tool that will show you all the popular searches.

Let me give you an example. If I type in "How to," Google will guess what I want and fill in the rest of my sentence. Here is what Google predicts when I type in "How to":

How to tie a tie

How to write a cover letter

How to boil an egg

Learn to Watch Trends

However big or busy you become, never allow yourself to get out of touch with what's going on. This includes developments in your industry, new technology, and up-and-coming businesses. To be successful, you need to know what's going on in the world, what people are thinking, what they are buying, and what they are concerned about.

It's pointless burying your head in the sand. You need to be ready to ride the wave of any new trend, because if you ignore trends, the chances are you'll get washed up.

Take the example of the New York Stock Exchange. It used to be where everyone traded stocks. Now, most trading is done by computer, and very few people actually trade in person. The New York Stock Exchange Floor is really a museum with just a few people left. Those still trying to trade this way are failing, because they haven't kept up with the changing world.

I have always liked to keep up to date with technology and the latest trends, and although it's impossible to know every new product, it's important to have a good overview of what's out there.

By watching trends and noticing how the world is changing, I have benefited greatly. Let me give you some examples.

1. I have made a great deal of money in the cellular phone industry, thanks to watching the trends. I was probably the first person to realize that a cellular phone (which were car phones in the early days) could be given away free and still generate profit.
2. I made extra income by using a premium rate number (0898, 1-900) when these first became available. People paid money to listen to a sales message, and I profited from this new technology.
3. I made money in the CD-ROM multimedia industry, both directly and by investing in other companies, when this technology was brand new.
4. By finding cheap freelance websites, like http://www.fiverr.com, I've cut my costs and made my life easier.
5. I've made millions from the stock market by looking at trends and investing in growth sectors. I don't always get it right, but all I need are one or two big trends, and I'm in the money.

Who knows how much I will gain in the future from new technology and trend watching? As I write, I'm watching some exciting new trends.

Sometimes, people say to me, "You're lucky, you must have been in the right place at the right time." This is total rubbish. I am certainly no luckier than anyone else, and the only reason I'm in the right place at the right time is because I made sure I was there.

By watching trends, *I put* myself in the right place. You can and should do exactly the same thing. No doubt, people will tell you how lucky you are—but you'll know different!

Nothing happens until something moves.

—Albert Einstein

Magic Words That Will Help Your Business

Here are a few magic words that will help your business, especially when you're starting out:

"Do you mind if I ask you a question?"

and

"I wonder if you could help me with a problem?"

Most people—especially older, successful people—want to help others. As the new kid, you're not a threat, and many people will be happy to help you. As a matter of fact, part of the reason I wrote this book was to pass on my skills.

If you're writing an e-mail, "Can you help me?" or "Can I ask you a question?" are not bad headlines to get your e-mail opened.

The Dangers of Having Too Much Money

If you're starting out with plenty of money, you'd better watch out. Having too much money in business is worse than having a limited starting budget. Let me explain.

Many big companies and government bodies throw money at problems, rather than finding an intelligent and noncostly way to avoid the problem in the first place.

Large amounts of start-up capital make you lazy, complacent, and comfortable. I started out with very little capital, and many other successful mail-order and direct marketing millionaires did the same.

Having low capital is the best way to start any business. Not having much money will force you to investigate and research all the possibilities before you let go of that limited cash.

If you *do* have a substantial amount of start-up capital, put it somewhere you can't get to it. Force yourself to work within a tight budget, where every penny is crucial. You will make fewer mistakes by working like this.

Take, for example, advertising agencies and the big-budget ads they produce and place for big clients, like motor car manufacturers. I'm sure you've seen the double-page spreads. What a waste of time! Anyone with half a brain could have produced a good ad on a single page.

Why two pages? Because advertising agencies want clients' money and can demand a bigger budget for a double-page ad. You'll notice when car companies are in financial trouble these double-page ads are the first thing to go.

If you're starting out with a limited budget or are living in poverty, consider yourself lucky. Being poor is one of the best motivations for success. When you're broke, you really don't have anything to lose, but everything to gain.

Think about it. What's the worst that can happen—you go to jail? Well, at least you'll get three meals a day and a roof over your head. Okay, that's a bit extreme, but my point is—think about the risks versus rewards. You'll almost always find the risks are worth it.

What People Want

This is a timeless list of what people are interested in. I first wrote this list over 15 years ago, and while technology has changed, people have not. Nor, in my opinion, will they.

People are basically self-centered and respond to appeals that promise gratification of some personal or intimate aspect of their life. These gratifications include improving their status, increasing their income, and gaining admiration, love, and success.

I have spent a great deal of time researching and looking into what people want out of a product or service, and I've listed my findings below. When I write a sales letter, e-mail, or website, I'm always focusing on these hot-button categories.

Think about products and services that can be built around the following (which are listed in no particular order, as they're all winners):

1. *Earning money*. I don't know anyone who is not interested in this. After all, you're reading this book, aren't you?
2. *Improving health*. There are very few people who can say they're 100 percent happy with their health. Fitness products, diets, organic foods, and vitamins are all big sellers. Right now, we have an aging population, so staying healthy is an even bigger concern.
3. *Saving time*. Everyone wants to do this. Who buys salad ingredients to wash and chop anymore? Most salad is now sold in pre-prepared bags.
4. *Being appreciated by others*. People like to feel special and wanted. They also like to receive compliments. What are social networks

all about, if not being appreciated? I treat my clients well. After all, without them I would be working at a fast-food outlet.

5. *Improving appearance and being fashionable.* Traditionally, the fash-ion world and skin care business have been focused on women, but these days the men's market is catching up. Fashion for the over-55s is also a growing market and a big money maker. Another trend is plus-size men and women's clothing.

6. *Avoiding criticism and pain.* Remember I said earlier, sell cure not prevention? People will spend more money on curing a problem than preventing it.

7. *Avoiding losing money or possessions.* People want to protect what they've earned (e.g., their home or car).

8. *Leisure.* The leisure and tourism markets are massive. With more and more visa restrictions being lifted all over the world, this is a boom industry right now.

9. *Improving social status and getting promoted.* People will pay to learn new skills: e-learning, seminars, and events are all money makers. Offering classes on anything from cupcake baking to photography can be very profitable.

10. *Attracting the opposite sex.* This one is never going to go out of fashion. Dating services and books relating to relationships will always sell.

11. *Avoiding work and/or effort.* No one wants to admit it, but we can all be lazy at times. Why do people pay to have their car washed? Or for pre-chopped vegetables and salad? It's not that we don't know how to do it—we don't *want* to do it.

12. *Security and comfort in old age.* This concern starts later on in life. No one wants to end up in a state-run nursing home. Remember, the population in the United States and Europe is getting older. Many advertisers are still focused on young people, but the real spending power is in the grey dollar or pound.

If you dig deep, you will no doubt be interested in some or all of these 12 categories. Have a brainstorming session and think about what you can provide that meets one or more of the above needs. I have just thought of one while writing this list—travel services for the mature traveler!

On the subject of travel, I often ask people at my seminars: "If you had all the money and time you needed, what would you do?"

"Travel" and "write" are nearly always the top answers. Sounds like a great product idea for an eBook or article titled: "How to be a travel writer" or "How to travel the world like a prince on a pauper's budget."

18

The Ideal Mail-Order Product

THE IDEAL MAIL-ORDER PRODUCT should be fairly small, lightweight (posting an elephant is expensive), not too fragile, and not available in local stores. Most importantly, the product must have a high perceived value and offered at 100 percent markup or more. In most cases, the typical markup will be 500 percent.

Let's look at that pricing.

A lesson I learned very quickly is that selling your product too cheaply is always worse than selling it for too much. It's a mistake most new businesses make. They think because they are new in business, they should work on small margins. This is not the case.

Let me ask you a question. If you needed a heart operation, and could choose either a U.S. $250 doctor or a U.S. $15,000 doctor, who would you trust? I would go for the most expensive one. Price and quality have a psychological connection. Many people believe that if it's cheap, it must be rubbish.

I'm not saying you should sell a paper clip for $500, and you need to make sure your customers are happy and believe they have received excellent value for money. However, you can always go down in price. It's much harder to increase a price that's too low, than decrease a price that's too high.

Let's pretend I'm selling a new home-study course. You inquire, and I send you my sales letter, which offers the course at $697.77. Now let's

148

say you don't respond to the offer. I can then write or e-mail with a new sales letter, offering a special LAST CHANCE price of $367.77.

Remember, it's not about how many products you sell. It's about the profit you make. You know the old saying, "turnover is vanity—profits are for sanity"? It's true.

In many cases, it's easier to sell one product at $297 than 10 at $29.70.

Lead-Generating Products

Although I favor high margin and higher-priced products, we can also sell different products at different price points—a bit the way airlines do. You can have an entry-level product (economy class), a more expensive option (premium economy), and then a premium service (business/first class).

If you're selling an e-book at $1, you won't make much after Amazon takes its cut, but if that $1 product is a lead generator, and at the end of the e-book you have your contact details and offer other services, then you start to make money. This is called backend selling, and I will talk more about this later on.

On the subject of backend selling, check the back of this book— you'll find contact details and websites that allow me to sell more products. You can't say I don't practice what I preach!

Tax

When you price a product, remember sales tax in the United States, or VAT in the UK. It's likely you'll have to register for VAT if you are trading in the UK and your turnover (not profit) is going to be over a certain amount per annum.

By registering, you will have to add a percentage to the price of your goods, which is then passed on to HM. Customs & Excise—normally every quarter. Basically, you're collecting taxes on behalf of the government, which isn't really fair, but you don't have a choice.

The good news is that if you're VAT registered, you can claim back the VAT you pay on business expenses. For example, if you buy a computer for your business that costs £1,000, you'll be able to claim back around 20 percent of this.

Completing tax returns can sound daunting. However, as long as you keep good up-to-date records, you'll soon find it easy. You can file online and will find a lot of free information—especially if you're a new or small business.

Remember—tax money isn't yours, even though it may be in your bank account for a while. If you sell something for £120.00, including VAT, make sure you don't count the £20.00, because it doesn't belong to you.

> NOTE: The VAT rate in the UK is 20 percent at the time of writing, but this could change in future. The current rates and thresholds can be found at http://www.hmrc.gov.uk/vat/.
>
> In the United States, have a look at http://www.sba.gov for current information—especially about e-commerce sales tax.

Selling Products You Like

It's important that you enjoy and understand the product you're selling. Why? Because it's hard to be enthusiastic about a product you don't like. I personally wouldn't like to sell clothing or cosmetics. I may invest in those companies, but I don't sell these products because I can't get enthusiastic about them.

At the same time, I must warn you about selling products just because you like them. Make sure you research your profit margins and market. Your hobbies do not always make good businesses. Remember, we are doing this to make money, not entertain you.

Specific Products

Some of the best mail-order products are information products. These includes books, how-to manuals, correspondence courses, self-improvement courses, newsletters, DVDs (training/seminars), spoken word CDs (self-improvement/spoken books), and computer software/peripherals. Let's look at information products in more detail.

Information Booklets, How-To Guides, and Manuals

People pay good money for information. Not so long ago, I sold a four-page document for £50. The ink and paper cost me less than 50p, but the customer greatly valued the information on that paper.

Here are some of the top-selling information topics:

How to make money

Diets/fitness

How to attract the opposite sex

Money-saving tips

How to win at gambling

Computers

Self-defense

Cosmetics

Remember to look at what's already selling well on Amazon or eBay. You don't need to be the first.

Producing a How-To Manual

You have three choices when it comes to writing a how-to manual.

1. Write and research the manual yourself. Let's say you choose "How to pick winning racehorses" as your subject matter. You can research the manual by collating information from the Internet, magazines, and books and by interviewing people. You can then format the guide yourself.
2. Pay a researcher to find out the information and produce you a script.
3. Find an existing manual on the subject, then purchase the reprint and resale rights, or enter into a wholesale agreement to buy the manuals.

Now, how will you sell your manual?

1. Use Google AdWords to discover how people are searching for your topic. In our case, people are searching for "make money from horse

`racing," so this keyword phrase is useful in finding our target market. We can then invest in pay-per-click ads to bring our audience to our product.

2. Place small ads in newspapers or online sites that carry horse-racing details.
3. Obtain lists of people who have bought similar products, and write to them. In the UK I have used the same list broker, Hilite, for over 20 years. Visit: http://www.hilitedms.co.uk, and yes—they do have lists of race horsing gamblers. In the United States, I have used http://www.namebank.com and http://www.macromark.com. Search for "direct mail list brokers," and you'll find plenty.
4. Advertise or do a joint venture with other websites.
5. Take on affiliates. Clickbank allows you to be an affiliate and sell other products, but you can also be a vendor and allow others to sell *your* product. The beauty here is Clickbank does all the admin, pays your affiliates, and checks for fraud while you retain your percentage of profits. So you can have an army of sales people selling your e-book course and only pay on results.

Audio Information

Anything written on paper can be put on a CD or digital download MP3. Today's time-starved consumers are willing to pay for information on CD; the success of audio books proves this.

Audio information can be put together very cheaply. A CD can be produced for 0.50 cents (0.30 pence) and the original master, including using a professional voice-over artist (depending on length), can be created for a few hundred dollars.

You can also record the audio yourself, with podcasting or audio software, which can be downloaded free or at low cost. If you do this, buy a good-quality microphone. I like the RODE podcaster—search online to find out more.

You can also buy the rights to a printed product and turn it into an audio product. This allows you to instantly charge more for essentially the same product.

Remember, you can outsource anything these days. Never think, *I don't know how to make a CD master*, because it's easier than ever to pay someone else to do it for you.

Did Bill Gates write MS DOS, (that's the early computer operating system before Windows) for you younger folk? No. He paid someone else to write it and licensed it to IBM. The rest is history.

DVDs

I don't mean making big budget feature film DVDs—no. I'm talking about creating low budget information movies. The success of YouTube should tell you how popular information videos have now become. There are some things that are easier to explain with real life demonstrations.

Let me give you an example. A friend of mine runs a U.S. company that cleans computers and offers other business maintenance services. The market for his services is very large, so he decided to make a low-budget video showing people how they could start their own business doing the same thing.

From a desk in his own house he demonstrated how to clean computers. He then explained how he markets his business and what he charges. His video was made with the help of a friend as the cameraman, and a simple home video camera.

To go with the video, he produced a short how-to manual and workbook. The manual, video, and workbook cost him only U.S.$10 to produce, yet he sells the whole package at U.S.$127 (£90).

The last time I spoke to him, he'd sold over 10,000 copies of his course, via mail order. Now, in case you're not too good at math, that's over $1.2 million!

Simple ideas like this work. Notice the high profit margin and how by only selling 10,000 he still made a lot of money. If he'd been working on a smaller profit margin and sold the package for $30, he would have had to sell over 40,000 videos to make the same amount.

In one of the courses I sell, "Making Money from Financial Spread Trading," I include a workbook and two hours of DVD footage showing how I trade. This makes my package more valuable than just selling a book.

It also means I can use small parts of the DVD as a teaser on YouTube to promote the full package. Many of my clips have over 50,000 views. How much did those views cost me? *Zero*. YouTube is free.

Figure 18.1

Who needs start-up capital? I use a free program to cut a few minutes of the full DVDs I own the rights to, and upload them at no charge to YouTube and other video sites. See Figure 18.1.

You can also make money recording seminars/conferences on video. For every person attending a seminar/trade show, there are probably ten others who couldn't make it or didn't want to spend a large amount of money attending the seminar.

Imagine there's a national seminar for doctors, and it costs $1,000 to attend. You could arrange to video that seminar and sell it to the list of doctors who didn't attend. You can even sell it to those who did attend!

Later, I will tell you where to find global trade shows and exhibitions.

Getting DVDs Produced

DVDs cost more than audio CDs. However, they can be sold for more, and costs are coming down. You can make a simple video at home, using a video camera.

For seminars, you'll probably need two video cameras, extra lighting, and a professional microphone. The footage can then be edited on a home PC, or you can rent a video studio with an operator. Again, editing and so forth can be outsourced. For a really inexpensive way to do things, look out for local colleges or universities with audio/visual courses. They may help you for a negligible fee.

You can sell footage by digital download. However, many people still prefer an actual DVD to be delivered to their home. I still deliver my financial trading course via physical DVD.

You can also use YouTube and other video sharing sites to show a clip of your video, then refer people to a site where they can get more details and buy the full DVD.

Video search is very powerful, and you *must* use video to promote your product or service these days. Google owns YouTube, and gives websites with video more priority, so if you want to be highly rated in search engines, make sure you add a video to your site.

Most people have heard of YouTube, but other video sites include Vimeo.com, dailymotion.com, and viddler.com.

Making a Video with PowerPoint or Keynote

A simple way to make a training or information video is by using a screen capture program. There are a few of these, the best-known being http://www.camtasia.com.

What is a screen capture program? In a nutshell, it records a video of what you're doing on your computer screen. You can also include audio, so if, for example, you capture an onscreen PowerPoint presentation, you can record your speech while you're presenting.

What might you make a video about? Well, perhaps you're good at using a certain piece of software. In this case, you could make a tutorial DVD. Or maybe you're good at playing online poker. You could create a DVD about making money from online poker, and capture your computer screen as you play. I use screen capture for my online trading, and show my clients how I use a certain charting program.

Webinars

Webinars can either be offered free as a lead generator/sample, or you can sell access to a webinar. Check http://www.anymeeting.com—a site offering webinar software for meetings of up to 200.

Anything that can be done in a traditional seminar can be done over webinar, and your members can vote, ask questions, and so on.

If you really want to utilize webinars, it may be worth attending a training course on television presenting. I attended one—not because I wanted to be a TV presenter, but because I wanted to learn how to present my DVDs and seminars. These courses can also help if you are ever interviewed on the television or radio.

The course I attended was run by http://www.pozitiv.com in the UK—nice people who know a lot about TV and media, and are reasonably priced. If you're in the United States, search "presenter media training."

The Internet is including more and more video content, and it's a trend you need to move with. You can set up your own Internet TV station for just a few hundred dollars, and this can be a very powerful selling machine.

Buying the Rights to a Video

I own the rights to 26 videos at last count. Most of these videos were purchased from the United States, and I edited them, converted them, repackaged them, and sold them in the UK and Europe.

Anyone reading this can buy the rights to a video and do the same. Most of the videos I own are how-to videos, which I package together with a book or a manual.

How to Buy the Rights to a Video

The first step is to get hold of the video and its sales letter. Choose a video that *isn't* on sale in your country. Next, identify the market you think would be interested in the video. Look at ways in which you can improve the video—can you add a workbook, help sheets, or computer software? What do you think of the title? Could you improve it and make the video more marketable?

Once you've decided to sell a video, you need to contact the copyright holder and explain what you want to do and how it will benefit them.

You could either make a one-off offer for the rights to sell in your country, such as U.S.$1,000, or you could offer a small advance of say U.S.$250 and a percentage of the sales—perhaps 5 percent of the sale price on each video.

The chances are that Joe Smith, the copyright holder, has never even thought about selling the video outside his home country. If you offer to sell it for him, you're essentially offering him bonus money.

If the copyright holder is in the same country as you, you can still buy the rights. There are many saleable videos sitting on shelves collecting dust—including some of mine.

Contact the copyright holder and make them a reasonable offer. You'll be surprised how many will agree.

Newsletters, Blogs, and Membership Sites

A newsletter or small magazine is a very good way to get into the media business. Today, many newsletters are delivered online, which makes profit margins even larger.

Most people are totally unaware of the vast profits and multibillion-dollar empires that have been built up through publishing books, newspapers, magazines, and newsletters.

Some of the richest people in the world have made their fortunes by owning media companies, including television and radio.

Buying a television/radio station or newspaper costs millions, but you don't need millions to create a profitable newsletter or small magazine. All you need is a little time and a minimal amount of capital.

Newsletters and Subscription Sites—What Are They?

People will pay large sums of money to find out about a particular subject. Whereas newspapers and mass market magazines usually provide a broad overview, a newsletter provides specific information on a particular subject.

Unlike most other forms of media, newsletters can be set up on a very low budget and produce staggering results. Let's say that you have 2,000 subscribers to a newsletter, paying U.S.$40 a year each. That's U.S.$80,000 a year! If you deliver a newsletter online, as I do, your costs are near zero. Even if you use the print and post model, you're still looking at less than $1 a month.

The big advantages of a newsletter are:

1. It can be started and run from home.
2. The technology to run a membership site is now much cheaper. A site like http://www.membergate.com makes it very easy to manage members, with no heavy programming.

3. You get paid up front. For example, if I sell you a 12-month subscription, and you pay me now, I don't have to deliver all at once. So technically, I'm getting an interest free loan from subscribers. Even if your clients pay monthly (which is now more common), you'll still have a steady monthly income. For example, if you have 500 subscribers paying you U.S. $19.97 a month, that's a nice monthly income hitting your bank account.

4. You have a residual value. Depending on how good your newsletter is, you will get renewals—so after 12 months, your income doesn't stop, it keeps going! A good newsletter membership should get around 80 percent renewals.

5. You can sell your newsletter and membership business when you've had enough, for a substantial amount. If you look at flippa.com you can buy and sell ready running websites—many already generating income.

6. There are many extra ways to make money, in addition to subscriptions. These include renting out your mailing list, carrying loose inserts, and showcasing reader offers.

Let me give you some examples of successful newsletters:

Competitors Companion   At one stage, this newsletter had over 100,000 subscribers—all paying around $70 a year. Well, 100,000 × $70 is $7 million! Even after running costs, such as printing and stamps and so forth, the newsletter still makes a massive profit.

What is this newsletter about? It's very simple. Every month, it publishes all the competitions open in the UK. The sort of information they give includes:

Where to get entry forms.

What the competition restrictions are, and if any proof of product purchases are required, e.g., three tokens from the side of a packet.

What the prizes are.

Closing dates.

Help with answers.

Sample competition slogans and tie-breakers.

Any other news the competitors need.

What a simple idea! The information is always changing, and it's free. The newsletter hires researchers who track down all the competitions, and that's it.

With the public's massive appetite for winning competitions, this newsletter will continue to grow.

Government Auction News   This is basically a monthly newsletter about where all the various auctions are to be held, what types of goods are available, and general buying advice.

And here are some other popular topics for newsletters:

Discount travel

Health and medical*

Finance and investments*

Food and wine

Computer newsletters

Accountancy and taxation*

Classic car

Model railway

Gardening

DIY

Restaurant owners

Why Everyone in Business Should Publish a Newsletter

I strongly believe that everyone reading this should publish a newsletter, no matter what business you're in. Even if you give the newsletter away *free*, you'll see great benefits.

---

* Notice: Any newsletter that relates to medical, legal, or financial advice must be written by a suitably qualified person. Take legal advice before proceeding. Investment newsletters must be regulated in the UK, but not the United States.

Figure 18.2

See Figure 18.2 as an example of a membership site, which was set up using membergate.

How to Make Money with a Free Newsletter or Membership Site

Making money by giving something away *free*? Are you sure? Yes. There are many newspapers in the UK that are distributed free. The advertising revenue pays for the printing, distribution, and staff's wages. Many of these newspapers are of good quality and make good profits.

Many television channels are free. Their massive overheads are paid for by commercials. When I ran TV stations in the UK, all our profits came from audience participation such as text messaging and phone ins. My channels were free to air, and we sold hardly any advertising.

Can a Free Newsletter Membership Site Work?

Yes, but advertising alone probably won't make your newsletter/ member site profitable enough. However, if you combine readers' offers and selling your own goods, it can be very profitable. Unlike a paid-for newsletter, your ads can sell a little harder to the subscriber, since readers haven't paid for the newsletter.

Offering a Free Newsletter/Members Site to Existing Customers

Imagine you own a computer software company, and Joe Smith buys your latest program. Instead of forgetting about him after you've taken his money, wouldn't it be a nice touch to offer him a year's free subscription to your computer newsletter?

This newsletter would include:

General computer news.

Updates about the software he has just bought.

Hints, tips, and details of our other products we have to sell— including upgrades.

The result? You'll sell more software to Joe Smith by sending him a free newsletter every month—more than if you'd sent him a sales letter. And that's how a free newsletter will make you money.

A newsletter doesn't cost much to produce or send out. If it's a free newsletter, you don't have to send one every month—it could be quarterly. Your newsletter can literally be one or two sheets of paper.

Keeping in regular contact with your customers is very important. Most companies take your money and forget about you, yet if they sent you a newsletter or catalogue on a regular basis, the chances are they would get more sales from you and create goodwill.

NOTE: The accountants I use have their own newsletter, which contains all the latest tax news and so forth, and is sent to clients free of charge. This creates goodwill, keeps their customers informed, and their name to the forefront. Yes, they also have a website, but there is still something powerful about receiving a printed newsletter.

How to Create a Winning Newsletter

What makes or breaks a newsletter? The topic. Pick the right topic and everything else will fall into place. Remember the hungry crowd? That's what you need for a newsletter. The crowd doesn't have to be massive, but there needs to be an appetite for your topic.

Now, you must market your newsletter. In fact, you should put around 80 percent of your efforts into marketing your newsletter, and 20 percent writing it.

Summary

A newsletter or membership site is a very profitable home business that can be started with little up-front money. A newsletter is also an ideal product to sell alongside your existing profession/job. Your membership site can also contain video and audio information.

Buying and Selling Websites

Today, real estate is more than just bricks and mortar. Real estate can be a website and/or a domain name. Many people make good money from buying and selling websites, and there is a very active resale market.

You can buy and sell domain names, too. A domain name I own (tradeonmarkets.com) was originally registered by someone else. However, they didn't renew it, so when it became available, I registered it in my name—which is perfectly fair and legal.

That $10 domain name could have been resold for at least $2,000. As it happened, I didn't want to sell it, but you can see the potential. So look out for domain names that are expiring. They could have a high resale value.

Some dropped domain names still have regular traffic and a Google or Yahoo search position. You can find various sites that list dropped domains—just search online.

You probably knew you could buy domain names, but did you know you can buy ready-made websites too?

Instead of setting up your own blog or finding a niche market, why not pay for a ready-made site? Visit http://www.flippa.com for details of websites for sale.

There are many talented programmers making software, apps, and websites, but 99 percent of them haven't got a clue about business or marketing. In many cases, programmers are totally broke. They have great products, but they don't know how to sell them. That's where you come in.

Contrary to what you might think, Bill Gates didn't get rich programming software. He's a billionaire because he's a great marketer. I read that for every 1 Microsoft programmer, there are 10 sales and marketing people. Apple struggled until they got their marketing right. Now, they're doing exceptionally well.

How about finding a good dropped domain name, building up a site, regenerating traffic, and then listing it for sale on flippa.com? This is an excellent way to generate income.

A *great* tip: Look at sites recently sold on flippa.com. This will give you a clue about what you should be developing. I recently saw a celebrity gossip site sell for $5,000, and it wasn't that special—just a wordpress template. It had traffic, which mainly came from other sites, and a nice clean design, but it could have easily been put together for around $300.

Review Websites

Review websites can be excellent income generators. How do they work? Let's take the example of a pet product review site. This site would include reviews of pet products, food, and toys. You make money by selling these products as an affiliate. Many people searching on the Internet are looking for reviews, which is why sites like tripadvisor.com are so successful.

Novelty Items, Kitchen Gadgets, Health & Fitness, Jewelry, and Personalized Items

Watch a shopping channel, and within minutes you'll see jewelry, kitchen gadgets, DIY, or health and fitness products. Why? Because these products sell. If they didn't, these channels wouldn't waste airtime on them.

I've been involved in TV shopping and watched orders coming in live. This showed me exactly what worked and what didn't. The TV channel would change formats, pricing, and products in response to viewer calls and orders.

One of the best salesmen/direct marketers in recent years has to be Ron Popeil—better known as RONCO. His products include kitchen gadgets and time-saving devices. His top tip is to make sure any direct marketing product can be sold as a gift. Without Christmas, Mother's Day, Father's Day, birthdays, weddings, and so on, most retail stores would go broke.

I recommend getting hold of Ron's book, *The Salesman of the Century*. This book is a few years old now, but it's still relevant. Ron Popeil explains how he went from selling kitchen products on a market stall to being one of the biggest direct advertisers in America.

You can still watch infomercials on YouTube.

Another very successful business to learn about is GuthyRenker (http://www.guthy-renker.com). You may not recognize the name, but it's the firm behind big sellers like Tony Robbins, Personal Power, Victoria Principal Secret, and Windsor Pilates, to name a few.

Seasonal Items

Let's face it—people spend more money around the holidays. How can *you* make money? Here's an example.

Halloween is popular in the United States and Europe. Around Halloween time, take a $3 pumpkin, add a face with some stickers, a nice tag, maybe some recipes, and a little story about the pumpkin. Your $3 pumpkin has become a gift that can be sold for $4.99 or more. Not a bad mark up. You may not be in the pumpkin business, but my point is that ordinary vegetables can be transformed into higher margin products.

Think about what you could source, and how you can enhance it and resell it. Many people buy items on eBay and resell them back on eBay at a higher price.

Don't be put off seasonal items. You can rotate, as most retailers do—sell Christmas pullovers during the holidays, then swimwear in the summer.

Products That Solve People's Problems

In direct marketing, any products, guides, or services that solve problems are big sellers. If you have a product that solves a common problem, the customer will not even think about the price. Remember—many people search online to solve a problem (for example, "my dog won't stop barking").

Let me give you a few examples of problem-solving products.

The problem: Chopping food and preparing vegetables is difficult and time-consuming.

The solution: The Chop-O-Matic. It cuts and slices food thinly in seconds, with no mess.

The problem: A diamond necklace is very expensive and impractical.

The solution: Fake diamonds, such as Diamonique. Affordable jewelry that looks good and costs very little.

The problem: Back pain.

The solution: A massager that straps to your chair and vibrates. The ideal gift for someone who suffers from back pain.

Research people's concerns, then provide a solution. This will give you an excellent chance of success.

Packaging Products Together

This is a very simple way to make a new mail-order product from existing items. Here is a true example of a wacky idea that became a big Christmas seller.

For years, confectionery manufacturers have taken a few bars of candy, put them together in a pretty Christmas box or stocking, and added 50 percent to the price.

One year I thought—what about a Christmas stockings for cats and dogs? All I needed was a cheap Christmas stocking and some small dog and cat treats. Many of the goods I chose for the stockings were sample/trial sizes, which were obtained from the manufacturers for nothing.

I put a nice printed card at the top of the stocking, with a picture of a cat/dog and a name tag, and the product was complete.

By taking existing products and putting them together, I made a new product.

On the subject of pets (and as a cat and dog owner, I speak from experience), pet owners are suckers and spend far too much on our furry friends. As a business, something related to the pet market makes a lot of sense. People often spend more on pet gifts than on presents for family members!

Internet marketing guru, Frank Kern, made a lot of money from an eBook called *How to Get Your Parrot to Talk*. Was Frank a parrot expert? No. As far as I know, he has never owned one. However, he is a good marketer. Frank noticed people were searching the term, outsourced the writing to a parrot expert, then did what he did best—marketing.

Some years ago, someone published a book called *How to Talk to Your Cat*, which also sold very well. If people are buying an e-book about talking to their cats, you don't have to be Miss Marple to work out that they're cat owners—meaning we can offer them other cat-related products.

I hope you're getting the theme of this section. To make money, you don't have to write or produce the product. Your main role is marketing and pulling it all together.

On the whole, people who make big bucks are not programmers, writers (two a penny), or cameramen—they're the people who pull it all together and do the marketing.

If you're selling a product, you can usually use just-in-time shipping, which basically means you have little or no stock, and buy products only when orders come in.

Back to Packaging Products

A very successful packaging concept was the introduction of music compilations. This was pioneered by a Canadian company, K-Tel, in 1970. Now, Telstar, Soundsdirect, Time Music, and numerous others all offer compilations. These companies approach record companies and pay them a set price and royalty, based on the hit status of the song. They then put the songs onto CDs or MP3 download, and sell through TV or radio.

This concept can be copied for many other products. I did this some years ago with a computer software CD-ROM.

Gift sets, hampers, and nicely packaged goods can all sell at a premium. Most men don't have a clue how to wrap a gift, so if you offer this within the sale, it's a great extra.

Importing and Exporting Products and Ideas

What do the following products and services have in common? Jeans, T-shirts, pizzas, pasta, popcorn, shell suits, home delivery of fast food, tool rentals, karaoke, and dancing Coke cans/flowers?

They were all ideas and products that came to the United States or UK from other countries.

The opportunity to import ideas and products from one country to another is enormous. Right now, Domino's Pizza is doing great in India. Yes, they've adapted the menu to suit tastes, but the concept is the same.

Whenever I'm travelling, I always look for products that can be resold in a different country.

Americans love things connected to the British Royal family, and also fine English teas and Scottish shortbread biscuits. Many expatriates based in the United States miss UK products, and vice versa. By shipping products from one country to another, you can meet a demand and add a nice markup.

Summary

Find products and services that people want and can be easily shipped. Choose products with high profit margins and perceived value. If you follow my guidelines, you'll have no problems finding successful mail-order products.

An old friend of mine, and successful author and businessman, Stuart Goldsmith, says: "People want to buy solutions to their problems, but because people are essentially lazy, they want the quickest and easiest route to do so."

Your job is to make life easy for your customers. It's also to make the world a nicer, more magical place. Your mailshot (website) and product should be as close to magic as possible (without lying), and as far away from cold, hard, reality as possible. People live in a world of cold, hard reality and are constantly searching for ways to evade it. Your product should help them escape the harshness of life.

Adding Value

A large box with a few extras in it gives the impression of more value. Let's say you're selling a set of kitchen knives. To add value, you could add a cookbook or a guide to using different knives. You could also throw in a few other small kitchen gadgets. Your price may be higher than just the knives alone, but the customer perceives good value.

I deal with an American company that always throws in a few extras with my order, like newsletters, brochures, mugs, and even baseball caps. This is an excellent way to help customers feel they have received good value.

Never get into price wars in business—the only winner is the consumer, not you. Pricing higher is actually a great way to add value to your product.

A Note on Copyright and Copying Others

There is a very thin line between learning from other people and *stealing* their ideas. If you take a book and copy it word for word, or duplicate a DVD without buying the rights, you are *stealing*. There's no other word for it. Don't do it. Aside from being morally wrong, you may get sued or even have a nasty visit from someone.

Be a Smart Copycat

Smart copycats read a book or ad, get ideas, and formulate a plan from other people's work. They then write their own book, or produce a video along similar lines. Nobody can copyright ideas or generic words like "at last" or "how to."

Take, for instance, supermarket-own brands. Their products are so similar to the brand leaders. Sometimes the packaging even looks the same. However, as long as the supermarket-own brands do not purport to be the actual brand, there is nothing the brand leaders can do.

Don't forget that you can be a *legal* copycat if you buy the rights to a product or purchase it wholesale.

Improving other people's ideas with a superior product, advertising campaign, or more appealing package can be a very quick route to success, and it's completely moral and ethical.

Why not buy this book wholesale, and package it with your own product?

What You Can Legally Copy—Public Domain

Public domain information means documents, videos, or books that for some reason have fallen out of copyright. This means you can reprint, resell, and make money from this information legally. Search "public domain information," and you'll be surprised what you find out.

People Buy People, Not Big, Cold Corporations

Before I go on, it's important to mention that people buy people. This means, to market effectively you must be a person. Use your name, a photo, and maybe a video. Customers want to see what you look like. Don't use fake stock people photos.

The future is people doing business with people—just like in the good old days of cottage industry. View customers as your friends and genuinely care. Big faceless, nameless corporations with call centers thousands of miles away are experiencing a big consumer backlash.

Make a feature of being a small business. Think niche and personal. If you look at Apple's recent success, it's because they have been very good at connecting with people in a human way. I-Stores are fun, bright places where no one hard sells.

Be ready to plug your business—don't be ashamed of what you're doing, or be shy. If you don't believe in your product or service, don't expect anyone else to!

19

Advertising and Marketing

BUSINESS IS NOTHING WITHOUT ADVERTISING and marketing. You can have the best product, the best letter-headed paper, and the best domain name, but if you don't know how to advertise and market your product or service cost effectively, you will fail.

I cannot stress how important advertising and marketing are. Imagine a successful business is a cake. Advertising and marketing is 90 percent of the cake.

Let me tell you the facts of life. *The best product* does not always win. The most successfully marketed product does. The winners are always the products the market likes the most.

Let me give you some examples.

Some years ago, there were two video systems—VHS and BETAMAX. Anyone who is technically minded knows that BETAMAX was the better product. In fact, BETACAM was used in the TV business until fairly recently. However, VHS won the consumers. Why? Because they won the marketing race.

How to Sell Today

Today's consumers are far more savvy and skeptical than they were 40 years ago. The hard sell, also known as "shout loud—money grab," simply doesn't work well any more.

Forty years ago, selling was all about the hard sell, and grabbing as much as you could, as quickly as possible. The theory was to money grab, by closing the sale as soon as possible for fear of losing the sale altogether. Salespeople were also taught to shout loud, that is, make a lot of promises.

This may have worked in the past, but today's consumers are turned off by brash selling. Don't get me wrong—I don't mind asking for a sale and writing persuasive copy, but it's not all about the quick kill.

Building Up a Relationship

I'd love to tell you that everyone who visits your website or receives your sales letter will get out his credit card and place an order immediately, but the world doesn't work that way. Today, depending on your product price, you're going to need to make at least five or six contacts before you get a sale.

In my business, I make first contact with customers by sending a free report, audio file, or blog article. I then contact again with a mixture of content and some sales message. This is building a relationship. Be a friend to your customer, not a salesperson.

Building relationships means long-term success. In my financial trading business, my customers are friends, and this means I want them to do well. Why? Because if my products work, they will spend more money with me and tell their friends. It's much easier to sell people your next product if they are satisfied with your first.

E-Mail Mailing List

I'm sure you've visited a website that asks you to register your e-mail address—usually in return for some free information. This is called lead capturing, and has been around for years.

Lead capturing is an excellent way to build relationships, as it lets you communicate with customers.

You can automate the whole process by using companies that offer various lead capture packages. Some good companies to try are: 1shoppingcart.com and awebber.com.

When you build your list of e-mail addresses, keep sales enquiries and customers separate, as you'll market to these two groups differently.

Using Lists in Offline Businesses

Let's say you own a restaurant. You can build up a list of customer cell (mobile) numbers and e-mail addresses, and contact them with special offers and restaurant news. If you know bookings are a bit light next week, you could send out a special offer e-mail or text message.

Here's a business idea. Go to your local restaurant and offer to help with their marketing for a fee. Then set up a system like this. Remember—most small businesses are not good at marketing. The chef may know how to make a great sauce, but I doubt he'll know much about Google AdWords and targeting.

Which leads on to . . .

Powerful Strategies to Boost Sales

No matter what business you're in, sales are your lifeblood. That may sound obvious, but some business owners get tied up in paperwork and red tape, and forget that without sales they have no business.

Irrespective of what business you're in, there are three primary ways to increase your revenue and sales:

1. Get more customers. Most businesses focus on generating customers, but in reality this may not generate much extra income.
2. Increase sales from existing customers. It's much easier to sell to existing customers than to a cold prospect. If you have ever bought anything from Amazon or eBay, you will notice that they e-mail you about new products like the one you just bought. You think that's an accident? It's important to create records of all your customers (buyers) and keep in regular touch by e-mail or post. Also, keep a list of enquiries and prospects, and follow these up. Most people don't go to your website and buy right away. In many cases, you will need to contact them three or four times to build up a relationship. Don't always hard sell in your communications. Offer some relevant information before mentioning a new product or service.
3. Increase the frequency of orders from your customers and increase your order value. In these economic times, many focus directly on price, but by adding value and packaging items you can often increase your order value and sales. Offer a standard or deluxe

package, and you will be surprised how many customers trade up to the deluxe.

Think about how you can also increase the purchase cycle. If customers order once a year, how can you get them to order every 6 months? Many dentists now ask customers to come in every 4 months for a check-up, not 12 months, to get at least 3 visits, and suggest a visit to the hygienist, too. Many hairdressers now make as much selling hair care products as they do from the haircut. If you have a captive customer in a buying mood, it's much easier to offer an extra. This can also be done online. If the customer is checking out, offer an extra product or upgrade.

Let's go back to the first point about getting more customers. It's important to monitor which marketing methods are working. Many spend thousands of dollars on advertising, but don't know whether it's of any benefit. Most customers don't buy on first contact. Your primary goal on first contact is to capture the prospects' details, and start the relationship process.

Of course in the age of spam, most clients don't give up e-mail addresses easily. You need to offer a bonus or benefit for parting with this valuable information. It could be a free report, special discount voucher code, free DVD, or other item that does not cost much.

Low Cost and Free Ways to Increase Sales

Write Articles and Post Them on the Internet   Let's say your business sells cameras. You can write an 800-word article about photography—a specific technique or new camera. At the end, add your details and website. This helps you build up credibility as an expert in the field, and also generates customer links. Sites such as http://www.articalbase.com and http://www.ezinearticles.com are great places to upload articles.

Become a YouTube Guru   With a basic video camera, webcam, or mobile phone, you'll be surprised how quickly you can make a professional-looking short video. Keep it to around three or four minutes, and give relevant information or tips.

For example, if you're an accountant, offer tips about doing taxes. At the end of the video, plug yourself and your business. Video is very powerful. Google (who owns YouTube) will rank video higher in search results than text websites.

I am a YouTube Guru for financial trading, with over 800,000 video views—and hopefully more by the time you read this.

Pixiwoo, who are makeup gurus, have over 123 million hits. They make money from their videos by promoting products, books, and courses and by selling advertising space.

Anyone can start a YouTube channel. Once you start building up views, YouTube will e-mail and offer you partner status (which I have), and you get extra privileges.

Start a Blog

Blogs can be set up for free and allow you to keep in touch with existing and prospective clients. Many perceive blogs as less threatening than sales websites. I would suggest offering good information on your blog, then linking back to your sales website. Try http://www.wordpress.com or http://www.blogger.com.

Personally, I like WordPress and have used them for years. You can get many plug-ins, which are free or low cost and allow extra features without having to write computer code.

The key to a successful blog is fresh and unique content. This keeps readers coming back, and your blog will rank higher in search engines if it has recent content. Copying content will do nothing for your online reputation—Google ignores it, and you may well get sued for breach of copyright. Of course, you can use small snippets from other sites, but it has to be relevant and sit alongside original content.

Link Swaps

Your competitors don't have to be your enemy. For whatever reason, your prospects may visit your website, but buy products or services from a competitor. By forming a joint venture or an affiliate link, you can still get some value out of the prospect and make commission.

For example, let's say you sell a course on fly-fishing, and the prospect has not bought your course. You can recommend other related products or books and earn affiliate commission. Amazon offers an "affiliate" facility that allows you to place affiliate product links on your website and earn money when customers buy.

Summary

Sales and marketing is a never-ending process. Put some, but not all, of your energy into finding new customers—it's much easier to make extra sales from your existing client list. The sales process should be about building a relationship, not just a one-off low-value sale.

How Compounding Made Me Rich

How did I go from near flat broke to multimillionaire? The power of compounding has a lot to do with it.

Let me explain more, but before I do, let me say that the technique I'm about to disclose has nothing to do with multilevel marketing, chain letters, or any other scam. It is totally legal and extremely simple.

Imagine you have a website bringing in $2 for every $1 you invest. Remember that many products will bring in far more, but let's stay with this figure to make things simple. Now, if you use your profits to double your investment, your profits will double too. Watch what happens to your income when you keep doubling:

1st time $2

2nd $4

3rd $8

4th $16

5th $32

6th $64

7th $128

8th $256

9th $512

10th $1,024

11th $2,048

12th $4,096
13th $8,192
14th $16,384
15th $32,768
16th $65,536
17th $131,072
18th $262,144
19th $524,288
20th $1,048,576

And that's how you can turn small capital into big results. I've used a small starting figure of $2. If you start with $5, then of course you will achieve one million quicker. I've also been realistic in my final figure—if you carried on doubling forever, you'd have to sell to the whole world!

How does this principle work on websites, small ads, or blogs?

Let's say you're running a small ad (could be online or in print) that makes you $10 a week profit, which is very realistic. Repeat the same ad in over 200 sources, and you'll make $2,000 a week.

Of course, all the while you should also be building your customer list for future sales (backend sales), meaning at one stage you'll also be able to sell higher-priced products to existing customers.

In the UK, I have around 15 small press ads a week, plus numerous online sources.

On the subject of compounding, it's also the way I became a multimillionaire from trading and investing. I started out with small amounts and rolled profits from one investment into another. I also used leverage, which allowed me to buy stocks with just a small percentage of the principal amount. For example, a $100,000 trade could be opened with $5,000. If you're interested in trading and investing, see details of my course at the end of the book.

Compound interest is the eighth wonder of the world. He who understands it, earns it . . . he who doesn't . . . pays it.

—Albert Einstein

Selling on eBay

eBay allows anyone to buy and sell. You don't need premises or merchant facilities—just a Paypal account, which is easy to open. Your marketing is done for you by eBay. Of course, they take a listing and selling fee, but these are low when you consider the service eBay offers.

When selling on eBay, focus on choosing the right product, and on creating good listing information (i.e., the description of your product, photos, and price).

I have already mentioned http://www.hotlister.com, which helps you find out what's selling well on eBay, and this research should be your primary focus. Of course, you can also test new ideas by listing products for a few dollars and seeing if they fly. eBay is a low-risk place to try new ideas.

Remember: The early bird gets the worm, but the second mouse gets the cheese. You don't have to be the first or only one doing something or selling a product.

eBay is famous for auctions, but just as important is its "buy it now" facility, which allows merchants to operate an online shop. In the past, most people went on eBay to pick up second-hand bargains. Now, it's full of professional sellers and is more like a department store.

I'll talk more about advertising and marketing shortly, but the keys to selling on eBay are:

1. Good photo (s) of what you're selling. Never list anything without a clear photo.
2. A good description of what you're selling. Use clear copy, full of features and benefits. Remember: the more you tell, the more you sell. You can also include video in your description.
3. Good feedback. This will take time to build up. Start making purchases on eBay to create good feedback.
4. Being honest. Yes, write persuasive sales copy, but don't lie. If something is slightly damaged, say so.
5. When you get an order, dispatch immediately. Nothing upsets buyers more than having to wait. As soon as you dispatch, e-mail buyers and tell them their product is on its way.

Amazon Marketplace

Amazon marketplace is almost identical to eBay's "buy it now" option.

You can either send your stock to Amazon for shipping to customers, or fulfill yourself. If you fulfill the order, Amazon will e-mail you when an order comes in. After a sale, Amazon collects the money and pays you, less their commission, after 21 days.

Even if you're running your own website, I still advise listing some of your stock on eBay and Amazon Marketplace, as they have massive traffic flow and rank very highly on search engines. Piggyback on their success, and you'll sell more products.

Remember, if you sell on eBay or Amazon you are given customer names and addresses for shipping purposes. This means you can sell other products or services to these customers, and you don't have to pay anything to eBay or Amazon for the privilege.

I sold a product on Amazon for £197, and they took 20 percent commission. A few months later, I sold a £2,497 product to the same client via a direct mail follow up. That time around, I kept 100 percent of the profit.

Selling on Clickbank

Clickbank allows you to sell digital information products online, such as e-books or downloadable video/audio clips.

Let's say you've written an e-book course called *How to Make Your Dog Stop Barking*. You can upload this product to Clickbank, build a sales page, and sell. As well as making your own sales, you also can have affiliates selling the product. Clickbank deals with paying commission and taking credit cards.

This is a very easy way to sell an information product.

Tip: When using Clickbank, make sure you create a video to promote your product. Videos can be embedded in the sales page website, so prospects can watch your video without leaving the page.

Spend some time researching what sells best on Clickbank. Various parts of the site show top sellers.

Promoting Your Product or Service

Trying to sell a product without advertising is like smiling in the dark. You know you're doing it, but no one else does! Good advertising will normally sell an inferior product, but bad advertising will make any product fail—even a good one.

Many people think if they put up a website or blog, people will automatically find it. Sorry—it doesn't work like that. You have to push traffic to your site, which is a continuous process.

Let's start by looking at newspaper and magazine advertising.

Although it's true that newspapers are losing market share, there are still many national and larger regional newspapers that are worth advertising in. It's interesting to note that many major online firms, like Google, eBay, and Amazon, advertise in newspapers and magazines.

Newspapers offer instant response. When my ads appear in a newspaper, I receive calls and Internet hits from 5 A.M. on the day of publication.

The downside is that a newspaper ad has a short life. If my ad is in Monday's paper, it will generate the most response that day, with a few more responses on Tuesday. After that, there will be very few responses.

Another downside is that newspapers are very general. Although you can target your market by placing an ad in a certain section (e.g., the business section), your product needs to be fairly general to work in a newspaper.

The newspaper ads I run are small box ads known as "two-step marketing." My ads invite readers to phone in (or these days, visit a website for free information) and ask more about the product.

Figure 19.1 is an example of two-step ads, taken from the UK Sunday Times business section.

You can track which ads work best by using a different domain for each ad. I use one domain for the *Sunday Times* and another for the *Daily Telegraph*. This way, I know which ad is getting the most responses.

I also use tracking scripts on my websites. Take a look at http://www.statcounter.com. This site gives you a small amount of code, which you add to your website. You can then use Statcounter's visitor statistics to find out where your visitors are coming from.

The U.S. and UK newspapers are fairly similar. Most have special days and sections. For example, Wednesday may offer a money section, and Thursday may offer travel.

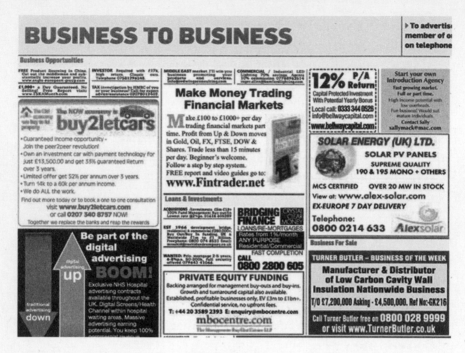

Figure 19.1

If your product relates to a special section, you should advertise on the day this section is published. For example, if your product is a "How to Cut Your Tax Bill" book, advertise on a money section day, or on the financial pages.

Profile

Financial Times and *Wall Street Journal* readers are different from *Sun* or *National Enquirer* readers. When selecting a newspaper to advertise in, it's important to understand the lifestyle and income of its readers.

Readers are graded into classes, according to occupation and other characteristics. Here are the broad marketing groups for newspaper readers:

A = managerial
B = professional

C1 = administrators

C2 = skilled/semiskilled laborers

D = unskilled laborers

These classes give some indication about reader lifestyles, levels of education, attitudes, and purchasing power—all very important factors when deciding which newspaper will best promote your product.

Media Packs and Sample Copies

If you contact the advertising department of any newspaper or magazine, they will send you a free sample copy of the publication and a media pack. The media pack contains their advertising rates and profile details. You can usually find these details online, too.

Before placing an ad in a newspaper, buy at least one week's worth of copies if it's a daily, or a few editions if it's a monthly.

If you read a daily newspaper every day for a week, you'll get familiar with the different sections and columns. You can then decide which day suits your product best.

Magazines

Magazines are great for advertising mail order. It takes longer for your ad to appear, but magazines have a longer life than newspapers. I keep magazines for months and even years, but I never keep a newspaper for longer than a few days.

Magazines are also left in doctor's/dentist's waiting rooms and offices and so forth, so they can end up being read by many different people.

The big advantage with magazines is that they are targeted. If you are looking to attract fashion-conscious women, advertise in women's fashion magazines, and so on.

Choosing the Right Magazine or Newspaper

Q: If you pick up a magazine and see there are no mail-order ads in it, should you advertise in that magazine?

A: No. It's better to follow the leader than be a pioneer. If a magazine carries mail-order ads, month in month out, you can safely assume those ads are working—otherwise advertisers wouldn't keep coming back.

Saturday's national newspapers carry many mail-order ads (buy a copy and see for yourself), so you can assume that Saturdays must be good for mail-order advertising.

The Sunday color magazine supplements are also full of mail-order ads—possibly because people are relaxed on a Sunday and buy more.

Summary

Matching the right publication to your product is very important. Spend time researching the various publications carefully. Good research will avoid costly mistakes. Watching other advertisers is the key.

I quickly learned that even with the best ad position, copy, and headline, I'd get little or no response if the publication was wrong.

Most magazines and newspapers now offer online advertising, too, and much of what I have said goes for online.

Start small. Run test ads before purchasing an expensive campaign. Try to negotiate a special test rate—I never pay rate card prices. If you're flexible, you can be put on a late space list, so if the publication has last-minute space, you can advertise at special rates.

Magic Words

Remember I said that words are magic? They are. Words can make you laugh, cry, smile and, most importantly, *buy products*.

The old rhyme, "Sticks and stones may break my bones, but words will never hurt me" does not apply to marketing. Get the words wrong, and you'll get hurt—financially.

Writing an ad, sales e-mail, sales letter, or website is called copywriting. Get the words right, and you'll make profit. Get them wrong, and you'll fail miserably.

If you're selling online, via eBay, Amazon, or Clickbank, you'll have to write sales copy for their pages, too. When you list a video on YouTube, you'll also need a good title and compelling text.

Over the next few pages, I'll give you a crash course in copywriting. This basic tutorial will hugely increase your chances of selling your product or service.

What Makes Someone Respond to an Ad?

In nearly all cases, it's the headline. The large-print words at the top of the ad are read first. If it interests the reader, he'll read the rest of the ad.

The headline is the appetizer or hook. It should be a striking statement, or promise some benefit. A headline needs to be effective in very few words.

> *On average, five times as many people read the headlines as read the body copy. It follows that, unless your headline sells your product, you have wasted 90 percent of your money.*
>
> —David Ogilvy

Strong headlines work for articles, e-mails, and blog posts, too.

Advertising Words That Work

Some of the words listed below have been used for many years, and may sound like clichés, but believe me—they work.

New, Amazing, Startling, Revolutionary, Miracle, The Truth, Announcing, Now, Suddenly, At Last, Last Chance, How To, Wanted, Easy, Free, Compare, Discover, Be A, Do You, Love.

Remember—people are basically selfish. They care about WIIFM— What's In It For ME. Your ad must tell them what's in it for them. If it doesn't, they won't investigate further.

Here are a few tried and tested ways to start your headline:

How to ... (one of my favorites)

Seven steps to ...

The secret to ...

Are you ...

An absolutely sure-fire way to ...

Should you . . .

Your guide to . . .

NOTE: If you're thinking of writing a book, manual, or marketing a video, remember the title is very important. I treat the title of my books and videos just like headlines. A good opening title for any book or DVD is, "How to"

Here are a few more great beginnings for book titles:

Seven secrets to . . .

100 ways to cut your tax bill

The complete guide to . . .

Be a highly paid . . .

Insider secrets to . . .

Confessions of a . . .

Everything you always wanted to know about . . . but were too afraid to ask

WARNING: Don't try to be clever in a headline. That's what advertising agencies do, and they normally end up killing the response. Your headline should be direct and easy to understand. Let's take an example:

HOW TO CUT YOUR HEATING BILLS NOW!

This is a very direct headline, with short, easy words.

I like to keep my headlines down to 10 or 15 words, maximum. In today's instant click culture, headlines need to be quick and snappy. This is often where expensive advertising agencies get it wrong.

Here is an example of an ad agency headline:

IF EVERY WIFE KNEW WHAT EVERY WIDOW KNOWS, NO HUSBAND WOULD BE WITHOUT LIFE INSURANCE.

This is a clever headline, but it will not grab the reader's attention. In fact, most people will not understand it at first glance. Do you understand what the story is?

The key to writing a great advert, sales letter, press release, website or sales speech is:

A = Attention. Grab the reader with a powerful headline or opening. People have a short attention span, especially on the Internet.

I = Interest. Keep your audience interested. Make the copy persuasive, yet informative, and make the copy believable. Back up any claims with research and testimonials.

D = Desire. Make them want to know more. Make them desire your product or service. You want the reader to feel that "this is what I have always been looking for," or "this is the answer to my dreams."

A = Action. Ask for action. Tell the reader to phone or click. Don't be afraid to insist that your reader do something.

The First Paragraph

The next step to a good ad is the first paragraph. We need to keep people reading. This means getting them excited, worried, curious—whatever it takes to spark their interest. Here are some examples of great first paragraphs:

Did you know that thousands of men and women are making $500 a week plus, working from home in their spare time?
or
It's hard to believe, but true—you're currently wasting thousands of pounds in tax benefits, because you simply don't know how to claim what's legally yours!

Body Copy

The main copy, also called the body copy, comes next. This is where you list all your product facts and benefits for the reader. The body copy needs to be easy to read and believable to sell the product. It should explain how your product or service will benefit the reader, and it must back up these benefits with facts.

Don't talk about you or your business. The reader doesn't care. It's pointless to say, "My company is the best, we've been in business for years, we're the biggest..."

The reader will say, "So what?"

Remember, people are reading your ad to find out, WIIFM. No— this isn't a new radio station. These letters stand for What's In It For Me, and they should be burned on your brain.

In an ad, people need to know *benefits*, such as:

The stainless steel chopping blade makes it simple to chop quickly. Easy to clean, and will stay sharp forever, saving you time and money.

Superwax polish gives your car a long-lasting, showroom shine. Easy to apply within twenty minutes, it goes on and comes off so easily, leaving you more time to drive your car, instead of polishing it.

See how these examples offer benefits to the customer?

If your ad is full of, "WE ARE...," then scrap it and start again. It should be full of, "YOU WILL..." A good rule of thumb is to make sure there aren't many of the following words in your ad: "I, We, My, Our."

A quick point about the length of body copy. You can never have too much copy, but you can have boring copy. As long as your copy isn't boring, write as much as space will allow.

I often see full page ads with 10 words in them—what a waste! It's been proven time and time again that copy is just as important as pictures, when it comes to getting ad responses.

Long text copy can be made to look interesting with the right layout, appropriate paragraphs, and bullet points.

If you use photos, write small captions underneath or beside them. Some people won't understand what a photo is trying to represent, unless there is text. A caption will help reinforce the photo's message.

Sales letters or websites can have longer copy, but in an ad (where you usually pay by the inch), space is a premium. Pay-per-click ads offer even less space for body copy. You usually have only three lines of text to get your message across.

Lots of copy is good, but make sure it isn't too cramped. A good way to check this is to check your ad at the end of the day, when your eyes are tired. If you find it hard to read, your potential customers will too.

Closing Copy

This is the action space. It's amazing how many ads or websites don't ask for action, or try to close the sale. Even if you're not asking for money or commitment at this stage, you still need your reader to act. Here are some examples of good closing copy:

Phone now for your FREE 24-page report, which reveals the tax secrets you should know.

or

Take action today. For the special introductory offer of only $19.95, you too can enjoy the benefits of...

Don't be afraid to tell the reader what to do next.

More Killer Headlines for Ads, Websites, and Online Marketing...

1. Announcing (Announcing a Breakthrough in...)
2. Secrets of (7 Secrets of the Millionaires)
3. New (A New Effective Approach to Losing Weight)
4. Now (Now You Can Have the Body You've Always Dreamed Of)
5. Amazing (You'll Feel Amazing after Using the "Relaxer" for Only 2 Weeks)
6. Facts You (Facts You Need to Stay Healthy)
7. Breakthrough (A Breakthrough in Pain Relief)
8. At Last (At Last a Diet That Really Works)
9. Advice for (Advice for All Aspiring Millionaires)
10. The Truth of (The Truth of How Vitamin C Can Prevent Heart Disease)
11. Protect (Protect Yourself from the Stock Market Crash)

12. Here (Here Is the Latest Money Making Offer)
13. Discover (Discover the Path to Riches Used by Millionaires)
14. Do You (Do You Want to Be a Millionaire?)
15. Bargains (Don't Miss These Hundreds of Bargains)
16. Yes (Yes! You Can Have the Figure You've Always Wanted)
17. Love (You'll Love Making Heads Turn When You're in a Jaguar)
18. How Much (How Much Money Can This Book Save You in Taxes?)
19. How Would (How Would You Spend Your Winnings?)
20. This (This Is the Only Tax Shelter Guide You'll Ever Need)
21. Only (Only Read This if You Want to Become a Millionaire)
22. Sale (The Greatest Sale of Ferraris Ever)
23. Hate (You'll Hate to Miss Our Latest Offers)
24. How To (How to Write A Book and Sell A Million Copies)
25. Free (Free Donut for Every Customer!)
26. You (You Can Have the Car of Your Dreams)

Pay-Per-Click Advertising (PPC)

I have already mentioned Google AdWords—the most popular pay-per-click advertising service. However, there are others, including Bing/Yahoo!, Facebook, and LinkedIn.

No matter what PPC program you use, the basic principles remain the same. Pay-per-click allows you to place a small ad (featuring a link to your website) on a popular webpage. Your ad appears when people search for certain keywords. When you set up your ad, you are asked to list keyword phrases you'd like associated with your ad. When people search for these phrases, your ad will appear.

You don't pay anything for your ad until someone clicks through to your webpage—hence the term pay-per-click.

Search YouTube.com, and you'll find many videos showing you how to get started with AdWords and other pay-per-click services.

The key to pay-per-click is not the amount of traffic you get, but the quality. It's better to use longer, more specific keywords such as "make money from the stock market" than generic ones like "make money online."

Search and Display Networks

In pay-per-click terms, "Search" means that when people type in a specific search keyword, your ad comes up beside the search engine. "Display" means your ad is placed around content—many times with a dubious connection to your product.

As you get more experienced, you can look at specific display locations. However, to start with, select only "Search" in your pay-per-click account.

Tracking Ads

Pay-per-click ads can be tracked, so you can follow responses and measure effectiveness.

Online advertising is still evolving, but it's worth learning about it and keeping up to date. You can start with a fairly small budget and set a daily spending limit—for example, $10.

Summary on Advertising

There is much more to learn about advertising and copywriting than I've shown you in these few pages. However, if you stick to the guidelines, you'll have a far better ad than most—and certainly better than any advertising agency could produce.

I have listed some of my favorite books on advertising on my website themillionairedropout.net, and I suggest you invest in them. You can never know too much about advertising and marketing. It should be your main focus in business. It is an area in which you must excel. I will post more updates and videos on my site.

20

Become an Expert by Writing Articles and Press Releases

WRITING ARTICLES IS A GREAT way to get free publicity. I have written hundreds of articles relating to financial trading, and at the end of each article I write:

> Vince Stanzione is the author of *Making Money from Financial Spread Trading*. To find out more go to http://www.fintrader.net.

This effectively plugs me and my products.

Normally, you won't get paid for these articles (although occasionally you may), but you *will* build up credibility and promote your business.

Another great way to build credibility and trust is to write a regular column for a magazine or newspaper. If you build a big enough audience, you may even end up on a TV or radio program.

In the UK, a start-up website called moneysavingexpert.com was propelled to stardom when it was featured on BBC Radio 2—a popular national radio station with millions of listeners.

The site's founder, Martin Lewis, became the moneysaving expert on a lunchtime call-in show. This promoted his website, for nothing, to millions of people. Martin recently sold his website for a cool £87 million.

Press Releases

Press releases are a very effective, yet often ignored, form of marketing. Writing a good press release and sending it to the right people is often the quickest and cheapest way for any business to generate publicity. You don't need a PR department to write press releases—it's quick and simple to create them yourself.

What Is a Press Release?

A press release is a story or announcement about your company, often relating to a newsworthy product. The idea is to get a journalist to write an article based on your press release.

The key is to provide an interesting story and plug your product somewhere within that story. At the end of the press release, you place your contact number, e-mail, and web address.

Journalists don't like people trying to sell things, so your story has to be strong. Your product plug within the story should be very small, otherwise your press release will end up in the bin or spam folder.

When you write a press release, it should read like an article in a newspaper or magazine.

For example, instead of writing, "I am the Director of ABC Computers and I would like to announce that I have invented a new laser printer," you would say, "Fred Smith, the Director of ABC Computers, has invented a new laser printer."

If you need help writing a press release, consult a PR consultant/ agency, or ask a local newspaper journalist to write the press release for you. Most journalists are underpaid and happy to take on freelance work. Try searching online for "freelance PR writers."

The Nuts and Bolts of a Press Release

A good press release should answer:

Who—Fred Bloggs, ABC PLC, the B&B Partnership

Where—London, New York, Bristol

What—New Car, Computer, Travel Service

Why—To help small businesses, to save energy

When—Now, open on January 1, 2014

How—Details on how to get more information and the stores selling the product

Identify magazines, newsletters, websites, and newspapers whose readers are specifically interested in your product or service. I don't send press releases about my financial trading course to knitting weeklies!

Wire Services

A wire service is really a distribution service. You upload your press release, and the wire service sends it to relevant media outlets (which you can select). There is a charge for this, so it may be worth trying once your business is up and running, but if your press release has good newsworthy content, a few hundred dollars in wire fees can earn you thousands back in free advertising.

Take a look at http://www.prnewswire.com/. While you're there, you can read other press releases to get ideas and see how they should be formatted.

Summary

Press releases are useful for any business and a great way to plug new products and services for *free*.

You can send a press release to newspapers, radio stations, TV stations, and Internet sites. Many authors have their books featured on the radio and TV. Indeed, radio stations often ask authors to appear live on air and chat about their books. This is great *free* advertising. Most media—especially live TV and radio—need to fill time with content. They *want* guests!

21

Why Back-End Selling Leads to Big Profits

IF YOU REMEMBER ONE THING from this book, remember this:

A one-off sale will make you money, but a lifetime customer will make you rich.

Here's the mistake many businesses make, both large and small. Joe Smith buys a book, DVD, or fishing rod from a company via mail order. Most companies fulfill that order, then forget about the customer. *Big mistake*!

The chances are that as long as you have supplied a good product and fulfilled Joe Smith's order promptly, he will be happy to buy from your company again and again. In fact, if a customer has bought from you once, you have just overcome his biggest problem—resistance to the first sale. Now that he knows you keep your promises and deliver promptly, he'll be much more likely to do business with you again.

How to Back-End Sell the Right Way

Firstly, when you ship the client's first order, send a letter thanking him for his order and enclose a catalogue or details of another product you

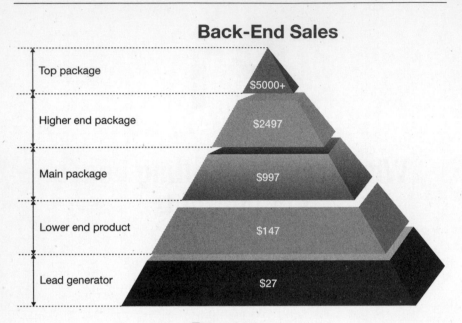

Back-End Sales

Top package — $5000+

Higher end package — $2497

Main package — $997

Lower end product — $147

Lead generator — $27

Figure 21.1

think might interest him. I also suggest sending a special voucher, offering a discount if he orders within 21 days.

If you don't hear from him, send another letter saying something like, "You recently ordered the XYZ course, and I would like to tell you about our new ZZZ video."

Alternatively, you could send a free newsletter, as previously mentioned. You could set this up to be automated via e-mail. However, with customers receiving more and more e-mails, this method is losing its effectiveness. A traditional letter in the post can still work well.

Build up trust and a relationship with your client. As you build up trust, customers will be happy to spend larger amounts. Be patient, though. Don't try to make love on your first date!

Figure 21.1 shows how you can have different products at different price points. A percentage of your customers will buy everything you offer, stepping up from $27 all the way to $2497 or $5000+.

Some customers will buy everything you send them details of. In a previous business, I mailed 30 different product offers to the same customer, and he bought everything. In fact, it got to the point where I just couldn't find anything else to sell him! Imagine if I'd forgotten him after his first order. What a wasted opportunity that would have been.

Find Another Golden Goose Before the First One Dies!

Let's say that you've developed or discovered a great mail-order product. The orders are pouring in, everything's on the up and up, and things are going great.

Remember—most products don't sell forever. Trends change, a competitor may start price cutting, and so on, and before you know it the Golden Goose is laying fewer eggs! The key is to have another product/service ready to roll out. It's rare that you'll be able to sell the same product or service forever. As previously mentioned, back-end products are what make real money.

However, don't drop a product too soon. Keep winning products going until they become economically unviable, and make sure you have another product planned for the slowdown.

Don't Be an Octopus

There is a temptation in business to start doing too many things at once, especially if things are going well. I call this the octopus scenario, and I've seen it many times. Yes—I want you to be ambitious and work to your full potential. However, don't get reckless or become a gambler.

If your business is a success, of course you'll want to expand and try other businesses. Just don't try to run 20 companies all at once—it won't work, and you may end up wrecking your first one.

Good Ways to Expand

Agents, licensing, and joint ventures are all good ways to expand.

Agents

I have recruited many agents, both in the UK and overseas, to sell products for me. Agents are a great way to employ a large sales force with no fixed costs. The agents only make money when they make a sale, meaning you only pay them when they make you a profit. I'm always delighted to write out big commission checks, because it means I've earned plenty of money, too.

Licensing

Virgin and Disney are very good at this. These companies both allow their name to be used on various products, and in turn they receive a cut. You can license or sell the rights to your products overseas.

Joint Ventures

Sometimes, you don't want to take a big risk on your own. Or perhaps you have expertise in one area, but are lacking in another. A joint venture can be a good way to mediate a big risk or make up a missing skill set. Obviously, you have to pick your partner carefully.

On a smaller scale, I have done deals with loose competitors, where I have sent out their sales material with our orders and vice versa. A 'loose competitor' is a firm which offers something similar or complimentary to what you already do. For example, you sell wine and another firm sells high quality bottle openers. Well, you could have an insert for them when you send out your client's wine order; any sales would get you a commission.

At the moment, many Internet companies offer links/ads to other websites, and in return they reciprocate.

Subcontracting/Using a Bureau

When I wanted to profit from premium-rate numbers, I could have gone out and leased my own lines, set up my own equipment, and received maximum profits per minute. Instead, I opted for a bureau. I subleased their lines, used their machines and expertise, and yes—I did receive a lower percentage per minute. However, I didn't have any start-up costs or long-term contracts.

Sometimes, it's better to take a smaller cut and not take on too much risk—especially when you're starting out.

> *Give me a lever long enough and a fulcrum on which to place it, and I shall move the world.*
>
> —Archimedes

Doing Business Overseas

There's a *big world* out there. If you use the Internet and reliable couriers, you can sell products and services almost anywhere.

Some products will need to be changed slightly when sold overseas. For example, if your product is a how-to manual, you might need both a European and U.S. edition. However, some products won't need to be changed at all.

As previously mentioned, I've bought many videos created for the U.S. market, and sold them in the UK and Europe.

You can get documents translated into another language relatively cheaply. You can also get audio recorded in Spanish or Chinese at very little cost.

Credit Cards Are a Global Currency

I have sold products to customers all over the world, and because I accept credit cards, there is no currency problem. A Visa card issued by a Spanish bank is processed just the same way as one issued in the United States. There are no currency problems, because the bank converts the funds for you.

The same goes with PayPal—it's a global service, and will accept and process almost any currency.

Your website will most likely be seen globally, so don't turn good business away by refusing foreign customers.

NOTE: Overseas freight and postage should be charged to the customer, as this can really eat into your profit margins. You may want to get a price list from the post office or courier for various countries.

Learning to Invest, but Keeping Costs Down

When you start making money, you'll probably start thinking about buying things your business needs—that is, investing. Let me share some advice:

1. I believe investing in technology and machinery and so on will usually benefit your business. However, anything you buy for your business must earn its keep. Don't buy something just because it looks good.
2. If you need to buy an expensive machine, consider renting it first, or taking it on a trial basis. You might also consider subcontracting the task to another company, or using a bureau.
3. Don't move into business premises until you absolutely have to. Save your money, work from home, and use a business center.
4. Buy nearly new or ex-demo items for business, and try not to buy the latest model if you don't need to (see Part III for more money-saving tips).
5. Always keep your costs to a minimum, even when you're doing well. Many people get complacent when they earn big sums, and start buying things like expensive business lunches, vanity ads, and full-price office equipment.

Remember—it's easier to save than to earn.

Apparently, Henry Ford offered $25,000 (a very big sum at the time) to any employee who could show him how to save a single nut and bolt on each automobile he made. Fewer nuts and bolts soon added up to big savings.

It was thanks to Henry Ford's penny-saving attitude that cars were produced at a price nearly everyone could afford.

Think about this example when you're running your own business. I've been able to save thousands of pounds in my business (which in turn meant extra profits for me) just by saving small amounts here and there. Saving money on little things, like envelopes, postage and paper, and so on (which most companies don't even think about) can lead to massive savings.

Part III will give you more ideas on keeping your business costs down.

When people start out in business, they tend to be very resourceful—usually because they have very little capital. Yet often, when they start making money, they become complacent and wasteful. Don't make this mistake.

Attending Shows and Events

Although we're in a digital age right now, shows and events are still big business. I have attended many consumer trade shows and public events, and they're great places for finding new contacts and ideas. It was thanks to the first computer trade shows that I was able to make money from software.

You can make large amounts of money by selling products at shows and events, especially if your product has a general appeal. Shows and events are also good places to test products and get instant market reactions.

Making Shows and Events Work for You

Here are a few tips for getting the best results from shows and events.

1. Identify the show/event target audience. Will they be interested in your product? It's pointless attending the Clothes Show Live Exhibition if you're selling a product relating to model airplanes!

2. How many people attended the show last year/last time? Is the audience big enough to bother with?
3. When booking a stand, try and get the best position you can, even if it means paying a bit extra. Location is more important than the size of your booth. Good locations are near toilets/restrooms and snack areas.
4. Have a practice run at home. Set up your booth to the exact space you'll have at the show. This will help you assess how your booth can have maximum customer impact.
5. Bring at least one person with you to help run your booth—preferably two.
6. Make your booth look as professional as possible. Use posters and display your product clearly. People need to know exactly what you're selling.
7. If your product can be demonstrated, make sure you do this, and bring a microphone so you can make a lot of noise and attract audience attention. Don't just sit there like a dummy. Make the effort to build up a small crowd. People are like sheep. If they see a huddle of people, they will soon flock around you.
8. Keep the price of your product at a round figure during a show or event. It makes it easier for people to pay in cash. Ideally, if it fits with your product, choose a price that can be paid with a bill—that is, $10 or $20.
9. Don't be afraid to price a little lower than usual. Shows are one of the few places you can make money with lower profit margins, because the volume is big and you don't have any direct mail or postage costs.
10. Have a jar where people can drop their business cards. You can build up great mailing lists at shows. A good way to get people's details is to hold a free raffle in return for e-mail addresses and phone numbers.
11. Have plenty of bottled water and a few snacks on your stand. It will be a very long day, and you'll need to stay hydrated.
12. Wear comfortable shoes. You'll most likely be on your feet all day.
13. Be ready for anything. Bring sticky tape, scissors, pens, markers, paper, and cardboard, so that you can make any last-minute signs.
14. Bring a cash box to put all the money in!

Want to know how to make money from shows and events without paying to exhibit? Let me tell you.

Let's imagine you sell products to engineering companies. First, identify a show or event where your potential customers will be exhibiting.

Attend the show as a guest, and bring lots of business cards and product leaflets. Give them out to as many exhibitors as possible.

Visiting 400 different companies, possibly all over the world, would be very expensive. However, attend a major trade show where these companies exhibit, and you can meet them all in one day.

Try to pick the quietest time of the show (normally the morning of the last day) to visit exhibitors. This way, you'll get more time to talk.

You can find out which shows and events are coming up, normally months in advance.

Selling products at a trade show or public exhibition can be a great way to make fast cash in a few days. Your main cost is the stand, but if you have the right product for the market, you'll make money.

If you are new to shows and events, start off by testing a few of the smaller, cheaper ones.

You can find lists of upcoming trade shows in the United States at http://www.tsnn.com. Also try http://www.biztradeshows.com for UK and global tradeshow details.

23

Summary to Making Money

THE KEYS TO MAKING MONEY are:

1. Form Your Own Business

    Whether it's part-time to begin with, acting as an agent, or consulting a few customers alongside your existing job, start your own business and be proud about what you do.

2. Put Customers First

    The aim in business is, of course, to make money. However, if you only focus on money without looking after your customers or finding out what the market wants, it's going to be very hard to make money. You must also genuinely enjoy your work, be proud of your business, and be happy to serve your customers.

    Some of the world's most successful entrepreneurs, including Henry Ford, Conrad Hilton, and Hoichiro Honda, believed that money was just a by-product of a good business.

    Realize that a one-off sale/order will not make you rich. It's repeat business that counts.

    Build up a relationship with customers. Be a friend, not a salesman.

3. Be Market Driven, Not Product Driven

    Find out what the market wants and who you can sell to *before* creating or buying products.

4. Create a Professional Image

Using paper with a good letterhead, a business center, and professional domain name will put you on a level footing with the big boys, even if you're a tiny company.

5. Don't Waste Money

Don't get suckered into wasting money in business. Negotiate everything and run a tight ship, even when things are going well. At the same time, realize that money invested wisely will improve your business. Invest in training, books, and seminars. It's pointless having state-of-the-art equipment if you lack the skills to use it.

6. Be Ready for Change

One thing in business is certain, and that is that there's nothing certain in business! Things change, often very quickly. Today's big seller is tomorrow's totally unfashionable item. Keep your eyes open, watch out for new trends and markets.

7. Don't Quit, Believe in Yourself, and Always Give 100 Percent

Stress, problems, new challenges, frustration, and letdowns are part of everyday business life. If you hide away in a corner whenever something goes wrong, you won't survive in business long. You'll get knocked down. It happens, and it's acceptable. The question is, do you keep bouncing back up again? You must bounce back, learn from your mistakes, and keep going. Stay on the ground for too long, and that's where you'll be forever. Get up, fight back, and you'll be a winner.

Everything is possible, and if you want something badly enough, you'll get it.

> *Keep away from people who try to belittle your ambitions. Small people always do that, but the really great make you feel that you, too, can become great.*
>
> —Mark Twain

8. Realize That Marketing Is the Key

No inquiries means no orders.

No orders means no money.

No money means no business.

No business means you're out on the street!

> —Vince Stanzione

The reality is that marketing makes or breaks you. You must advertise, use press releases, direct mail, the Internet, and any other method that will effectively spread the word about your product or service.

9. You Don't Have to Know It All

Remember—you can outsource most tasks, license products, buy resale rights, have someone else write a book for you, or research a product.

Thanks to the global marketplace and sites like http://www .fiverr.com, http://www.elance.com, and http://www.guru.com, almost any task can be outsourced at a reasonable price.

Remember—this section is just the beginning. To succeed in business, you must become a good student, as you will need to continually learn new skills and information. This book will get you started, but it's just a step on the road. There's a whole, exciting journey ahead, and one that's well worth making.

The information revealed in this section will allow anyone—even those with little or no business experience—to start making money the smart way. The tips in these pages will help you avoid the mistakes most start-ups make and set you on a path to success. This information, combined with your own hard work and perseverance, will ensure you'll be a winner in business. You can keep up to date at http://www.themillionairedropout.net where I post regular updates and links to useful resources.

In Part III, we'll talk about saving money and getting the biggest bang for your buck. Being a smart buyer and making your money go as far as possible is often overlooked in business—yet it's crucial to success.

PART

III

Saving Money

24

Saving Money

So far we've talked about self-development and getting in the right frame of mind for success. We've also talked about making money. Now I want to share the power of saving money and being a smart buyer.

When I tell people that shopping and buying is a skill, they usually think I'm crazy. After all, when you need something, you buy it—right? Yes and no. If you want to make the most of your money and maximize your spending power, you need to be a *smart* buyer.

I've seen people struggling to live on $250,000 a year, and others get everything they want and need on $50,000. What makes the difference? The way the money is spent.

How to Add Fifty Cents to Every Dollar

Once you learn to get the maximum bang for your buck, you will realize that by spending wisely you are effectively earning more money—but without working harder!

Now, I'm not saying that we should go and live on a park bench to save money. That's not a life style that you or I would aspire to. However, taking simple actions to save money can make a massive difference.

Do I Really Need It?

Before making a major purchase, think: *Do I really need this, or is it a fad or impulse purchase?* If you do really need it, consider the following options:

1. Could I rent it for the few days I'm going to use it?
2. Could I buy it and share it with someone else to bring the cost down?
3. Could I buy it secondhand, ex demo, or slightly used?
4. If I buy it and then sell it in X amount of time, what could I get back (depreciation)?

I'm sure you've made regrettable purchases in the past. We all have. However, by getting into the habit of thinking before you buy, you'll make wiser spending choices. Don't be pressurized into buying a special offer right now. Trust me—99 percent of the time, it will still be on sale tomorrow at the same price.

Also, don't be afraid to send something back for a refund if you've made a mistake.

Now that we've got the basics out of the way, let me show you some great ways to save money, get better value, and have fun along the way.

Airlines

Over the years, I've flown all over the world with many different airlines. I fly Business and First Class, and always get knockdown rates. You can get reduced rates, too. Here's how (for legal reasons, I can't name the airlines, but the following advice works with all the majors):

Don't Buy Tickets Direct   It's usually a bad idea to phone an airline's central reservation number or use their official website to book a flight. You'll rarely get a discount by dealing direct.

Why? Because airlines don't want to be seen as cheapening themselves by offering discounted flights. Instead, they sell leftovers or X fares at a discount to a consolidator.

Only book direct if the airline has a genuine sale on. These do crop up from time to time, and discounts are offered in all cabins, including

Economy, Premium Economy, Business, and First. When one airline has a sale on, another will often also have a sale and price match, so this can be a good time to buy a flight.

You can never know for sure when an airline will have a sale. However, a few websites, such as http://www.flyertalk.com, have discussion boards with good info.

How Ticket Codes Can Save You Money   These are the standard IATA codes:

R Supersonic or First Class Suite (currently only on the Airbus A380)
P First Class Premium
F First Class
A First Class Discounted

Business Class Category

J Business Class Premium
C Business Class
D Business Class Discounted
I Business Class Discounted
Z Business Class Discounted

Economy/Coach Class Category

W Premium Economy, Economy/Coach Premium or Economy Flex
E Premium Economy Discounted
S Economy/Coach
Y Economy/Coach
B Economy/Coach Discounted
H Economy/Coach Discounted
K Economy/Coach Discounted
L Economy/Coach Discounted
M Economy/Coach Discounted (Round the World Fare)
N Economy/Coach Discounted
O Economy/Coach Discounted
Q Economy/Coach Discounted
T Premium Economy Discounted or Economy/Coach Discounted
U Economy/Coach Discounted or Unreserved on shuttle flights

V Economy/Coach Discounted
X Economy/Coach Discounted

I travel in Business and First Class a lot. "J," "P," and "F" tickets will normally have a limo/car to and from the airport included in the ticket price. In First Class, "P" and "F" may also have a special drive-through check-in so you can bypass the airport. Very nice, but at a premium price. The premium tickets are also flexible, so you can get a refund and change the dates with little or no penalty.

At the other end of the scale, Business Premium "Z" tickets don't include a limo (no big deal) and only offer airport check-in—albeit at a priority counter.

You can prebook a seat online, and once onboard you are treated exactly the same as the other full-fare customers you're sharing a cabin with.

A "Z" ticket will also come with conditions. These might include booking the flight at least 30 days before travel, and staying abroad for a minimum number of nights.

On a recent flight to Canada, I paid £500 for a First Class ticket. This was only a little more than an economy ticket, yet it should have cost £2,800. How did I get this deal? By booking with a consolidator at a time of the year when First Class wasn't selling well.

Business and First Class seats are normally booked by companies and governments. However, there are certain times of the year when business travel is slow. For example, August in New York is normally a slack time for business, so you can often get great deals in Business and First. Christmas may be busy in Economy, but business traffic tends to slow down until around the second week of January.

Last Minute Is Not Cheap   It's a myth that booking airlines last minute gets you a better deal. Perhaps it was better to book last minute years ago, but these days booking late costs you more. You'll get the best deals by booking in advance.

It also pays to be flexible. Often, if you can change your travel dates by just a few days, you'll see a big difference in price.

Many routes to the UK around the first and second of January can be expensive, as people need to fly home for work. If you fly on the fourth or fifth, it can make a massive difference.

Getting Upgrades Even if you've bought an economy ticket, it's possible to get upgraded to Business or First Class. There are two ways to do this—the free way, or the paid-for way.

If you don't mind paying a little extra (but not full price), go to the airline ticket desk and ask about possible upgrades. Be as friendly as possible. It helps if you have a frequent flyer card (which is free).

Depending on availability, you may be offered an upgrade voucher, which is only valid one-way. Sometimes, you can use frequent flyer points to pay for the upgrade, or a combination of points and cash.

It helps to look smart when requesting an upgrade. Don't wear a camera around your neck and holiday clothes. Airlines don't want anyone in Business or First Class who could upset their full-fare paying customers.

What's the free way to get upgraded? It's not that easy, these days, but it's still possible. First, you have to be considered "SFU," which means "suitable for upgrade." This means you have to look like you'd fit in with First Class or Business Class cabin customers.

Then, you simply ask at the desk, "Is it possible to be considered for a courtesy upgrade?" If Economy is overbooked for any reason, you'll become first choice for an upgrade to Business or First. This method normally works best if you're travelling alone.

Another option, if a flight is overbooked, is to offer to be one of the passengers to take the next flight, in return for an upgrade. Often, the next flight will only be a few hours later, and the upgrade can be well worth the wait.

Arrive at the gate on time, but don't stand in line to board until right at the end. If the flight is overbooked, the gate agents offer upgrades to the people last in line.

Consolidators and Bundled Deals Sometimes it's cheaper to buy a flight with a hotel or car hire included. That's because heavily discounted flights are often sold as travel bundles.

I recently booked a flight and hotel together, at a much cheaper price than just the flight. Granted, the hotel wasn't great, but I'd got such a good price on the Business Class flight that I happily paid to stay elsewhere.

The Internet Isn't Always Cheaper   You might think the big Internet sites, like Expedia and Priceline.com, are the cheapest places to book flights. By all means try them, but remember that often travel agents will get you a better deal.

When buying from travel agents, always pay by credit card. This protects you if the airline or agent goes broke. Do your research, and make sure your agent is legitimate before booking. If you book via a consolidator, you can check your e-ticket number with the airline to make sure it's valid.

Consolidators change around so often that listing names here would be meaningless. However, there are current consolidator suggestions on my website (listed at the end of this book). You can also take a look at *Business Traveller* magazine.

Travel Insurance   Never buy travel insurance from an airline or travel agent. The price is always highly inflated. You are far better off buying a multitrip insurance policy that will cover you for a whole year. For U.S. residents, try http://www.travelguard.com. If you're living in the UK, Ireland, or Australia, try http://www.multitrip.com.

Hotels

Hotels work differently from airlines, and last-minute bookings can normally work in your favor. Most hotel owners/managers would rather fill a room, even for a low price, than have it sit empty.

How to Book   Check the hotel website and see what rates are available. You will often see an "enter a discount code" box on hotel websites. Phone the hotel and politely say, "I'd like to stay at your hotel for a special occasion, but I'm on a budget. Do you have any offers or discount codes available?"

You can also search the Internet for "discount codes offers," adding the name of your hotel.

Also, look out for new hotel openings. When a new hotel opens (or reopens after being closed for a while), it tends to offer special rates.

Getting the Right Room   Hotels have different rooms and configurations. You and I could both stay at the same five-star hotel, yet my room might be totally different from yours. Make sure you get the best deal, but be realistic. Measure your expectations against what you're paying.

If you're staying in a motorway hotel for $40 a night, don't expect the royal suite treatment. However, it should be clean, tidy, and fit to stay in.

If, on the other hand, you've paid a large sum for a five-star hotel, make sure you're not palmed off with a substandard room.

If you're not happy with your room, say so immediately. Express your disappointment and point out the problems. Ask to see the duty manager, if necessary, and explain that you are a frequent user of hotel review sites and will be making a trip review.

Websites such as Trip Advisor allow you to give a good or bad report on a hotel. No hotel wants a bad Trip Advisor report, especially if it includes photos.

Stay calm and don't be rude. However, be firm and explain your reasons. Most hotel managers will do whatever it takes to make you happy.

Loyalty Programs   Just like airlines, the major hotel groups have loyalty schemes. If you're a regular guest at a chain, it really does make sense to join.

Getting an Upgrade   Again, like airlines, hotels offer upgrades. You can pay for a better room, or ask for a complimentary upgrade. See what you can get for free first; then find out what's available for an extra fee. You will normally get a better deal by booking a lower grade room first—then buying an upgrade at the hotel. However, bear in mind that if the hotel is fully booked, you won't be able to upgrade.

Where to Find the Best Hotels in the World   Perhaps you have a special occasion coming up and want to stay in real luxury. For the very best hotels, visit the Leading Hotels of the World website (http://www.lhw.com). They often have special offers, such as three nights for the price of two.

How to Hold a Hotel Meeting/Get-Together for Free   Few people realize that you can use hotel facilities, even if you're not staying there. I have conducted many business negotiations in a plush hotel lobby or bar area. All I pay for are a few bottles of mineral water or cups of coffee. As long as you look smart and blend in, no one bothers you. You can normally use the various hotel facilities too, such as free wireless Internet.

Discount Car Rental

You'll be amazed at the savings you can make by shopping around for your car rental company and quoting the discount code/scheme references.

On the whole, I've found it cheaper to prebook cars rather than book at the airport. Unless you have a specific reason for hiring a big car, always book the smallest vehicle, then ask for a complimentary upgrade at the desk. Often, you will be given a better class of car than the one you booked.

Note: I personally stick to the larger, well-known car-rental firms, because I've had some bad experiences with local one-off companies. Their cars and service can be very poor, and often the price difference isn't worth it.

The Internet is a good place to hire cars, and you can use price comparison sites to find the best deal. If you rent cars regularly, consider getting a loyalty car.

Always shop around, and try to find discount codes. Search online for Hertz or Avis discount codes, and you'll often find some good reductions. Also, some credit cards offer special car-rental deals to cardholders.

Don't forget—if you're booking a flight, see if bundling it with a car rental can cut your costs.

Buying Electronic Goods

Although you can buy nearly everything online these days, it's still worth checking out retail outlets (the few that are left) and shopping around.

Managers Offers, Returned Goods, and Ex-Display   Big retailers offer money-back guarantees, and many people do return goods. The stores then sell them again—normally at a 25 percent discount or more, and they still offer a guarantee. Many online retailers also sell returned or end-of-line goods.

Buying a Slightly Older Version   Let's face it—there's always going to be a newer version of the latest gadget, but do you really need it? Say you want to buy the Apple iPad. The previous one or two versions will still give you everything you need, and normally at a great saving. Also, should you want to sell it yourself, you'll find the big depreciation has already happened.

Sites like http://www.ebay.com or http://www.ebay.co.uk offer a great marketplace for electronic goods, both new, used, and refurbished (returned). You will also find some excellent cell phone deals on eBay.

Tips for Buying on eBay

1. Check out the seller's feedback and reputation.
2. Read the small print, and carefully assess what's included (or missing).
3. Watch out! If the seller is overseas, will you have to pay VATs/Sales tax/import duty? If you're in the UK and buying from within the EU, you normally won't pay import duty. However, if you buy from the United States, you'll probably have to pay customs and excise before they release the package. eBay lists the latest rates.
4. If you're buying an electrical item from a foreign seller, will it work in your country, and has it been approved? If it's just a case of changing the plug or using an adapter, then no problem. But some electronic items won't work outside their country of origin, for various reasons.
5. If the deal sounds too good to be true, it normally is. If you're offered an original Gucci handbag at $20, then most likely it's a fake. eBay has put a lot of effort into stopping fake trading recently, but you still need to be aware.

Buying a Nearly New Car at a Discount

How would you like a nearly new car—normally no older than six to eight months and with all the manufacturer's guarantees—for around

30 percent off the normal price? It's possible to get deals like this, because major rental-car companies sell used cars.

Try http://www.hertzcarsales.com in the United States and http://www.hertzcarsales.co.uk in the UK. Elsewhere in the world, just search, and you'll find various companies offering ex-rental cars. What I like about Hertz is that they normally offer a few days to test the car. If you're not happy, you can have your money back.

The only small disadvantage is that the mileage may be higher than normal on an ex-rental car. However, this will average out if you keep the car a few years.

Another way to get a nearly new car at a great price is to look for ex-demo cars offered by dealers.

> NOTE: If you're not in a rush to buy, December is the best month to get a great car deal. People are thinking about Christmas and the weather isn't great, so business is slow for most dealers. Make a deal close to Christmas/New Year, and it'll most likely be a good one.

Buying Car and Home Insurance

Nobody likes buying insurance, but it has to be done. Here are a few tips for saving money:

Vehicle Insurance

1. Make sure you're using the right ZIP or postcode, as this can make a big difference to your premium.
2. If you're willing to meet the first $500 (£300) of a claim (known as the excess), you can reduce your premium. Decide whether the saving is worth the expense of paying out $500, should you make a claim.
3. If you are a low-mileage motorist, you should be able to get a lower premium. Also, if you're not using the car for commuting, you should get a reduced premium, too.
4. On the whole, buying online should get you a better deal. However, it's still worth giving local brokers a chance. Even with their commission added, they may still get you a good price.

5. Make sure you're grouped in the right occupation band.
6. Never lie on insurance applications, either on the phone or online, as it makes your policy invalid.
7. Watch out for price comparison sites, as many are, in fact, owned by an insurance company. They may not be as independent as you think.
8. Never accept a renewal without checking at least one other firm. If another firm quotes you less (and it usually will), you can go back to your existing insurer and ask for the client retention department. Often, this department will match the price of your new quote.
9. Make sure you're covered, but not paying for unnecessary extras.

Home Insurance   Much of what I have said above applies for home insurance. In fact, many firms will offer a better deal if you buy car and home insurance together.

Many home insurance policies offer block insurance coverage of say, $30,000 of contents. However, if your contents aren't worth that much, getting an individual quote to the exact value could save you money.

Office Products

If you're running your own business, you'll probably need office supplies. Make sure you get them at the best price.

In the United States, try http://www.officedepot.com. In the UK, try http://www.viking-direct.co.uk—they also have various European sites, including ones for Spain, Germany, and Poland. Just click on the flag for your country.

Normally, low-cost office suppliers offer next-day delivery on everything, so you can keep stock levels low. If you're a new business, you may also be able to get 30 days free credit.

25

Buying Designer Clothes for Less

THIS SECTION MAY BE MORE useful for ladies, but men can pay attention too. How do you buy original top labels from Chanel, Gucci, Prada, and Louis Vuitton, to name a few?

Dress Agencies

There are a number of excellent dress agencies that buy, sell, and exchange designer clothing. Most of the clothing has hardly been worn, and offers excellent value for the money.

If you have quality designer items that you no longer wear, then trade them in. You can receive cash, or more items. Of course, if you have nothing to sell, you can just buy at a great price.

Many agencies also sell accessories, such as shoes and handbags. Some agencies also have brand new stock, normally made up of samples, ex-fashion-show items, or last season's stock.

Here are some UK clothing agencies:

London Area

Pandora

16-22 Cheval Place, Knightsbridge London, SW7 1ES

http://www.pandoradressagency.com

Pandora is a very well-known agency, close to Harrods.

Sign of the Times Dress Agency

17 Elystan Street London SW3 3NT United Kingdom

Telephone 020 7589 4774

http://www.signofthetimesdressagency.com

This agency has been established for over 30 years, and is located near Brompton Cross.

You can find a list of other UK agencies at http://www.dressagency directory.co.uk, or just search "dress agency."

The London Designer Sale   The London Designer Sale is a high-end designer sample sale that hosts designers such as Belstaff, D&G, See by Chloe, Gucci, Ralph Lauren, Jimmy Choo & YSL (plus many more boutique and alternative fashion brands) at up to 80 percent off the RRP. It's mainly women's stock, but there is also some men's clothing.

There are usually four or five sales a year. Check http://www .thelondondesignersale.co.uk for the next date and venue.

Factory Shops and Outlet Village Shops

Many companies have shops at their factory premises. Obviously, you have to weigh up the cost of travelling to the factory, but bargains can certainly be had. Some factory shops only open one or two days a week, so check before travelling. Also—bear in mind that some factory shops only accept cash.

Factory stores also have sales—a bargain hunter's heaven!

An excellent UK factory shop for men's shoes is:

Church's Factory Shop

Off St James Road,

St James,

Northampton

Northamptonshire, NN5 5JB

Phone: 01604 593313

A good choice for UK china, crystal, and tableware items is:

Villeroy & Boch Factory Shop
267 Merton Road
London SW18 5JS
+44 (0) 20 8875 6006

If you find yourself in Aachen, Germany, and like chocolate, check out the Lindt factory shop, which sells for around 30 percent off the retail price. The Lindt website, http://www.lindt.de, lists other shops around Germany.

Inca, which is in Mallorca, Spain, is where Campers shoes are made and has a factory shop, which sells items like Campers shoes at around 40 percent off retail price. See http://www.camper.com.

Outlet Villages   Outlet villages are shopping areas containing a range of shops, and are popular in the UK, United States, and Australia.

An outlet village may contain anything from 10 to 150 shops, and you will spot many familiar main street names. Goods on sale are often end of line or those that were slow to sell in retail stores. You can normally spot the color and size that has not sold well!

Discounts in outlet villages aren't usually as high as those offered in factory shops, but great savings can still be had, in comparison to main street.

In the United States, http://www.outletbound.com has a very good directory of all states, and you can search by area or company name.

One of the best outlet villages in the UK is Bicester Village. See http://www.bicestervillage.com/.

Remember—if you have a good eye and spot a bargain, you can buy an extra few items and sell them on eBay.

TJmaxx (or TKmaxx in the UK) is also worth a mention. These stores sell women's, men's, and children's clothing and accessories. They also sell household items at great prices. There are many designer labels on sale. Look at: http://www.tjmaxx.com for the U.S. store, and http://www.tkmaxx.com for the UK.

Perfume and Makeup for Less

Perfume and makeup have big margins, thanks to all those flashy TV ads, and department store floor space doesn't come cheap. By all means, try out the products in the stores, but don't buy them there.

If you're looking for original, top-branded perfume and makeup try http://www.cheapsmells.com.

On the subject of makeup and face creams, many house brands, like those offered at Boots, CVS, and Walgreens, rank very highly in consumer tests, yet sell for a fraction of the brand price—so don't always rush to buy the big brands.

26

Buying from Auctions and Wholesale

AUCTIONS CAN OFFER REAL BARGAINS, and they sell all sorts of things, including cars, caravans, RVs, boats, and even tanks! If you're bold enough to bid, they're a great place to get a good price.

Government Auctions

Governments auction items that have been confiscated—often because they were bought with the profits of crime. Some items are also recovered stolen goods, for which a legitimate owner can't be found.

Don't worry. If you're buying at a legitimate government auction, you're not buying stolen goods. Anything you buy will come with full ownership paperwork.

General Auctions

General auctions sell off all sorts of things, including brand new stock, raw materials, and office equipment/machinery. Normally, items come from companies that have gone bankrupt.

General auctions also sell end-of-line job lots. Sometimes, manufacturers clear out seconds, end-of-line products, and mail-order returns from their warehouses by selling them at auction.

You may also find items that can be cleaned up and resold.

What You Need to Know

The best (and often biggest) auctions have no reserve.

A no-reserve auction means you can bid U.S. $1, and if no one else bids, the item is yours. Big auction houses don't have the time or space to hold stock—they just want to clear everything out. So you can get some real bargains.

Before you get carried away and bid U.S. $1 for some massive machine, remember it's your responsibility to take it away—normally within a limited time period. If you can't take it away reasonably quickly, you could be charged storage.

The best auctions happen on business days, not weekends.

To find out more about auctions it's worth subscribing to a newsletter like Government Auction News, which is UK-based. Also, visit http://www.ganews.co.uk to find out more about buying at auction. In the United States, the official government auction site is http://www.usa.gov. You can also visit: http://www.govliquidation.com. When buying at auction, remember that sales tend to be final. There are no refunds, and you don't always get much time to inspect the goods. *Note:* If you're buying a car at auction (or even privately, as a matter of fact), always get a report on the vehicle. In the United States, you can use http://www.carfax.com, and in the UK you can use http://www.hpicheck.com. The minor cost of getting a report could save you thousands if your car turns out to be stolen, written off, or have finance outstanding.

Buying Wholesale at Discount Clubs

One of the best wholesale discount clubs is Costco. This brand has gone from strength to strength in the UK and United States. If you're in business and have a letterhead or business card, you should be able to access wholesalers or specialist shops that sell to traders.

27

Getting Cheaper Calls

CALL CHARGES HAVE DROPPED DRAMATICALLY, both in the United States and the UK. However, cell phone calls can still be expensive.

In the UK, I use a service called 18866 (see http://www.18866.co.uk), which can be used from a landline or cell phone to make discounted calls. It offers great savings—especially internationally.

International Calling Cards

If you need to make international calls while traveling, try using http://www.pingo.com. All this prepaid service requires is some credit on your account. In most countries, you can access the service from any phone by dialing a local-rate number, and your call charges will be cut dramatically.

In many hotels, calls to local numbers are free. By using Pingo, you can make international calls without paying high hotel rates.

Skype

Skype is a great way to keep in touch when travelling, and it's free to contact another Skype user. They also offer discounted calls from Skype to landlines and cell phones.

Cable TV, Satellite TV, and Cell Phones

I've been involved in all three of the above industries, so I can tell you a few money-saving tricks of the trade.

Cable, satellite, and phone companies basically want steady cash flow, so they like getting you on contracts. They also like persuading you to add on extra services for a little extra a month. However, think carefully before adding services. Will you really use them?

Look at what you actually use, compared to what you're paying for. In many cases, you can reduce the package you're on and pay much less. Take TV, for example. People often pay for channels they never watch—especially since many channels are now available for free. In the United States, Free To Air channels are available in most areas. In the UK, Freesat and Freeview offer free TV.

All major companies have a client retention department. If you contact them when your contract is coming to an end, they'll usually offer you a better deal. Look to review your contracts at least every year.

In the United States, try http://www.myrateplan.com, which compares various media companies. In the UK, try http://www.simplify digital.co.uk for TV and Internet. For cell phones, try http://www .uswitch.com/mobiles.

At http://www.uswitch.com, you can find price comparisons on gas and electricity suppliers. However, always call your current supplier before switching, and tell them you're going to leave. They may make you a good offer for staying put.

Credit Cards, Cash Back, and Points

WHENEVER YOU USE YOUR CREDIT card, the merchant is charged a fee—of which the issuing card company gets a percentage.

For example, Marks & Spencer have a credit card. If you use it to buy a plane ticket, the airline pays a fee. M&S gets a percentage of the fee.

It follows that customers should get a little of the fee, too. In the case of M&S, you'll receive points when you spend, which can be redeemed in store for food or other goods.

This card has no annual fee and offers 55 days of interest-free credit (although cash advances are not interest free). So overall, not a bad card. If you're going to make the purchase anyway, you may as well get something back.

American Express has a Blue Cash Everyday card, which has no annual fee and offers cash back per spend. This card is available in the United States and UK.

Tip: Amex offers a business version of its Blue Cash card. This card includes cash back and extra interest-free days to pay.

Some cards also earn air miles. Personally, I prefer to get cash back and vouchers.

Which card you apply for depends on your credit status, but if you're in the United States see http://www.creditcards.com, as they have a selection of the best offers. In the UK, try http://www.comparethe market.com, which offers a good selection of credit card deals.

Need a Credit Card but Have Poor Credit?

To survive these days, you need a credit card. However, if you have bad credit, previous debts, or no established credit rating, getting a card can be hard.

Luckily, you can get a credit building card. These are special cards issued to customers with lower credit scores. They normally come with lower spending limits, but as you pay off the balance, they will increase these limits. Do be aware that if you do not pay off the balance in full, the interest rates on these cards can be very high.

Secured Credit Card

This is more like a debit card, but can work for people with low credit scores. Basically, you put money into an account, but cannot spend more than you put in. The advantage here is that you don't have to carry cash around, and you won't overspend. Just search "secured credit cards" in the UK. You can try http://www.capitalone.co.uk.

A final note on credit cards. Always check your statements. Many card companies have now switched to online statements only, so check the web each month. Make sure you recognize all payments, and check you haven't been overcharged or double charged.

Credit Card Offers

If you use Visa, MasterCard, or Amex, you can sometimes get extra discounts by paying with your card (regardless of your card issuer).

Try http://www.usa.visa.com/personal/discounts and http://www .marketplace.mastercard.com.

29

How to Get a Discount on Anything

THE SIMPLEST WAY TO GET a discount or a better deal on anything is . . . drum roll please . . . *ask*. It sounds so simple, but most people don't.

I'm not saying you should ask for a discount on a cup of coffee at Starbucks, but if you're making a major purchase, or are a regular customer, don't be afraid to ask for a discount—or at least see if you can get a few extras thrown in.

Recently, I bought a new suitcase. I checked various sources, and the price was roughly the same everywhere. I asked for a discount, but the sales assistant said the price was fixed. However, he included an extra smaller bag as a bonus. So just by asking, I got something extra. Even if you don't personally want an extra item, you can always sell it or give it as a gift.

Saving money, just like making money, is about being open and on the lookout for opportunities. Ask politely, with confidence, and a smile. You'll be amazed at the discounts you can receive.

Coupons and Discount Codes

Often, when you check out online, you'll see a promo or coupon code box. If you search for the code online, you may be able to get a discount or some free extras. Try http://www.myvouchercodes.co.uk.

Let's say you're ordering from Thornton's Chocolates. Do a quick Google search for "promo code Thornton's chocolates" and narrow your search by date. You'll want to find the most recent results, as codes quickly expire.

Gift Cards

If you have been given a gift card but don't want to use the store it's tied to, why not sell or trade it online? In the United States, try http://www.plasticjungle.com. In the UK, try http://www.giftcardconverter.co.uk.

Remember—if you're thinking of making a large purchase at a particular store, you can often buy a gift card at a discounted price. They're often sold at 10 percent less the face value—essentially offering $100 of spending value for $90. eBay also has an active market in gift cards and vouchers. I recently saw $100 of M&S vouchers sold for $89.

Fancy Seeing a Free Show?

Many TV shows are filmed with a live audience. This means you can watch shows for free. In some cases, they will even pay you a small amount for food and drink.

In the UK, try http://www.applausestore.com. They have all the top BBC, ITV and Channel 4 shows. At the time of writing, they also offered tickets in Australia, and are soon to launch in the United States.

The most popular shows go quickly, but you can be put on a waiting list.

In the United States, try NBC (http://www.nbc.com/tickets/). Also, visit http://www.tvtickets.com for details of many top shows, mainly filmed around LA. Another U.S. site for free shows is http://www.mytvtickets.com.

For BBC shows in the UK, try http://www.bbc.co.uk/showsand tours/tickets/. They also have some great radio and music events—all free.

Note: You should not be charged a fee, as the TV production companies pay the agency.

Remember, you can apply for tickets in a country you're just visiting. I was in Los Angeles a few years ago, and got a front-row seat at *The Tonight Show with Jay Leno.*

Eat Out for Less

All restaurants have quiet periods, and would rather offer a special deal than have tables sit empty. The key is to eat a little earlier or later than most, or choose days that aren't so busy. As you may know, restaurants make most of their margin on drinks, not food, so you can often make big savings on your meal.

In the United States visit http://www.restaurant.com. It offers great savings on eating out. Another good U.S. restaurant directory and booking service is http://www.opentable.com.

In the UK there is a similar service called http://www.toptable.co.uk.

If you're in the UK and like to eat out often, visit http://www.gourmetsociety.co.uk. You can get 50 percent off many restaurants. There is a card fee, but this can be covered in a few meals.

In London, the D&D restaurant group (which includes the Blue-bird, Le Ponte De La Tour, and Floradita) offers some great menu deals. See http://www.danddlondon.com/offers.

Many main-street restaurant chains offer two-for-one deals, especially mid-week, and you can find vouchers online. Try http://www.moneysavingexpert.com. They have an active community that shares information.

Also try http://www.myvouchercodes.co.uk and click the "restaurants" tab. They normally have offers on most main-street chains, such as Pizza Express.

30

Making Your Money Work Hard by Saving and Investing

I HAVE A FINANCIAL BACKGROUND and am successful in trading and investing. This book isn't about trading and investing (anyone interested in that area should look at my specific sites). However, I would like to give a basic overview of investing in the stock market without being taken for a ride.

Money makes money, or so the old saying goes. When you build up extra capital, you should make it grow.

Imagine what would happen if your money grew by 10 percent every year, thanks to clever saving and investment. This is a perfectly possible growth rate. If you started with $10,000, over five years your money would look something like this:

Year 1 $11,000

Year 2 $12,100

Year 3 $13,310

Year 4 $14,641

Year 5 $16,105

Of course, over 10 or 20 years, your money will look even better. The best part about simple investing is that it takes very little time.

How can your money earn you 10 percent per year? You don't have to buy or sell stocks or shares. All you have to do is buy low-cost index funds.

The truth is, even most professional investment firms can't beat the stock market average, yet they charge high fees for investing your money. You can do perfectly well on your own. Here's how:

1. Open a low-cost broker's account, such as http://www.schwab.com or http://www.etrade.com. In the UK, try http://www.tdwater house.co.uk or http://www.hl.co.uk.
2. Buy an index fund that gives you broad exposure to the stock market (so rather than picking shares, you're buying the whole market).

Your returns will match that of the index, less a small amount for the management fees (and we're talking 0.20 percent or less—no big 1 or 2 percent fees).

Use Up Your Tax Allowances

Depending on where you live, you should be eligible for some sort of tax relief on investments. For example, in the United States the 401K plan allows around $16,000. UK law lets residents invest around £10,000 a year, tax free.

I don't want to enter into the realms of tax or trading advice, but a basic overview will give you the pillars of being a smart investor.

Here are my key tips for saving money and making it work harder for you:

1. Don't try to beat the market—just buy the market.
2. Keep costs to a minimum.
3. Pay as little tax (legally) as you can on your gains.
4. Don't pay for expensive investment advice, hedge funds, or pension funds.
5. Don't fall for Ponzi or get-rich-quick schemes.
6. Whenever you have extra savings, buy more exchange-traded funds (ETFs). You can buy each month or quarter.
7. If you're paid a dividend, reinvest it.

Realistically, think of investing over 7 to 10 years, and don't worry about whether the market is up or down today.

Keeping Some Cash in Savings

You should always keep some savings readily available—that is, in an instant access savings account. Although interest rates aren't great anywhere right now, it's better to get something than nothing on your savings.

In the UK, look at some of the smaller building societies. These often offer better rates. However, you normally have to deal online or by post, as they don't have many branches.

There you have it. My very quick and simple tips for investing in the stock market. For those wanting to learn more about trading and investing, check out my site, http://www.fintrader.net.

Summary

Learning to spend and invest wisely is the key to maximizing wealth and making your money last. No matter how big you get in business, keep a tight lid on expenses and you'll keep more of your income.

Many people say that because I'm rich, I don't need to haggle or get discounts. The truth is, wise spending helped me accumulate my wealth in the first place.

I'm not a miser. I enjoy spending my hard-earned money. However, I also ensure I get the best deal I can. This way, I can have my cake and eat it!

Even after all these years, I still get tremendous satisfaction from discounts, free upgrades, and special bargains.

Learn to take charge of your money by investing. It's not as hard as many experts want you to believe. Understand that the power of compounding can make a small amount of money grow over time. Don't expect the government or state pension system to take care of you in your old age. Take charge of your own destiny.

I hope you've found enough good advice in these pages to more than cover the cost of this book.

I will be regularly updating links on the book's website, so make sure you check http://www.themillionairedropout.net.

31

Time to Say Goodbye—Where Do We Go from Here?

WE'VE COME A LONG WAY together, through the course of this book. Pat yourself on the back and congratulate yourself. If you use the information revealed here, you will soon be on an incredible journey and enjoying an amazing lifestyle.

Now that you've finished this book, you have the knowledge to get you started. However, I urge you to put the knowledge into *action*. You truly have everything to gain and nothing to lose.

This book draws on years of my experience, and I urge you to reread it and use it as a reference. Don't just put it on the shelf and forget about it. Make it part of your life and success story.

Let me take this opportunity to wish you all the success and happiness in the world, because you truly deserve them. My sincere thanks for letting me share this life-changing information with you.

Vince Stanzione

Free Newsletter and Updates

You can keep in touch and up-to-date by visiting my website: http://www.themillionairedropout.net. Here, I will regularly add new audio files, videos, and generally share my experiences with you. It would also be great to hear back from you, so please feel free to add your comments and ask any questions via the site.

Index